RICHARD WURMBRAND
THE MAN AND HIS WORK

by *Merv Knight*

*"Never judge a man
until you have walked a mile in his shoes"*
– Indian proverb

RICHARD WURMBRAND
THE MAN AND HIS WORK
By Merv Knight

Second Australian Edition, October 2009

ISBN 978-0-9587431-4-3

Printed and published by Stephanus Publications (Australia)

Published for Voice of the Martyrs
PO Box 250, Lawson NSW 2783, Australia

INTRODUCTION

For me it has been a journey so far of 40 years. It is not a journey I sat down and planned. The journey began when my friend and co-worker Reg Werry put a copy of *Tortured for Christ* into my hand in 1968 and recommended I should read it. Reading the book, and a year later meeting the author, set me, together with my wife Grace, on a lifetime journey. As I write these words the journey is not over, and although there have been both rough and smooth places, there are no regrets. This small book began decades ago in Britain as a few pages compiled by Grace Endall who has long since gone to be with the Lord. Encouraged by Voice of the Martyrs colleagues around the world, and by the original author's mother, it has been my privilege to add to the text and bring the account of Richard Wurmbrand's ministry into the twenty-first century. The task is not finished. The road on which we joined Pastor Wurmbrand stretches on ahead. The church is persecuted and there remains much work for us to do.

"And let us not lose heart in doing good, for in due time we shall reap if we do not grow weary. So then, while we have opportunity, let us do good to all men, and especially to those who are of the household of the faith." Galatians 6:9-10.

– Merv Knight

FOREWORD

Voice of the Martyrs, Servants of the Persecuted Church

The Voice of the Martyrs (VOM) represents God's answer to Pastor Richard Wurmbrand's prayers during the fourteen years he spent in eight prisons in communist Romania.

A main emphasis of the mission is to be what its name implies – to be the voice of the martyrs – being a voice for those who, otherwise, the world would never know about. Apart from this, the efforts of VOM are directed towards helping Christian martyrs and their families in restricted nations. While the ministry continues to give help to struggling believers in those nations that have emerged from decades of Marxist rule, its main thrust is to serve those who face persecution today under Islamic, communist and other oppressive regimes.

In some countries Christians are in prison for their active faith, or they are discriminated against because of their Christian beliefs worked out in their lives. This Mission helps by sending material and spiritual help – sometimes using secret methods.

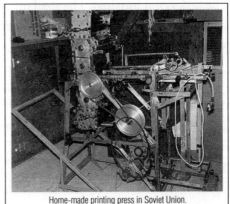

Home-made printing press in Soviet Union.

The Mission smuggles Bibles and evangelical literature into some remaining communist countries. This is done by using couriers, by balloons, and by other clandestine methods. In some countries literature is printed secretly in large quantities and at great risk. For four years Communist authorities of a certain Soviet town tried to locate a secret Christian printing press, but without success. All searches of suspected homes and premises were of no avail until, at last, through betrayal, the secret press was uncovered. It  was located in the basement of the State Security Service (KGB) office building and approached through a secret tunnel accessed down a drain. Here a large quantity of Christian magazines and books were printed. In times past, literature was dropped from the air or floated in packages on the sea to the shores of countries hostile to the Gospel. Similar activities continue today.

In Eastern Europe and what used to be the Soviet Union, where enormous changes have occurred, advantage has been taken of the new openness to supply the churches with Bibles, Christian literature and other forms of practical help.

Since the partial decline in international communism through the 90s, a surge of Muslim, Buddhist and Hindu militancy has occurred. This opposition to the propagation of the Christian Gospel created a vast new field of need and opportunity for the ministry of Voice of the Martyrs and its sister missions.

In Australia, New Zealand, Europe, the United States, Canada, South America, Britain, Scandinavia, Asia and South Africa, VOM spreads the message of the persecuted church that suffers under godless regimes, and alerts free men of their own peril. This is done through the mission newsletter, with DVDs, books, special advertisements, literature, interviews, by speaking at meetings, use of the internet, and any other valid opportunity that is available.

The Good News for tightly guarded Albania. One of our mission's Italian co-workers demonstrating how thousands of Gospel portions and Christian pamphlets, sealed in plastic, were launched on the Adriatic Sea. The currents washed them ashore.

THE CHARACTER OF THE WORK

The work of this interdenominational family of Missions stands firmly upon the inspired, inerrant Word of God. Its diverse ministry is international, evangelistic and constructive. The prayers, interest and gifts of Christians sustain and enlarge the work through the power of the Holy Spirit.

CRACKS IN THE IRON CURTAIN BEGIN

Since 1967, when VOM was founded by Pastor Richard Wurmbrand and his family, we have seen many changes. In the early years of its existence, Voice of the Martyrs worked by stealth and creative planning to bring Christian literature and aid to the underground church, in nations that were under the heel of communist rule. The work was both difficult and dangerous – as it continues to be in many areas of ministry today. These early years were our first attempts to create cracks in the iron curtain that was separating East and West.

I first met Richard Wurmbrand in August 1969. For those who remember it, I waited with several friends in the old Sydney Airport international terminal, situated near to where the Qantas domestic terminal now stands – T3 as it is known.

Nearly a year before this day, after reading his book *Tortured for Christ*, we had written a letter inviting him to come to Australia and New Zealand for meetings. So moved were we by the book that we wanted to give people in Australasia an opportunity to see and hear the man in person.

The story began when a student at the Ambassadors for Christ Illawarra Bible College at Stanwell Tops, a few kilometres south of Sydney, gave a book to the registrar, Reg Werry. In Reg's words, "One day a young man, one of my students, approached me and asked if I would like to read a book which had been a great blessing to him. The title intrigued

The original book read by Reg Werry.

me – *Tortured for Christ*, by Richard Wurmbrand. I read it through at one sitting and God opened my eyes to the fact that a great host of my brothers and sisters in Christ were literally being tortured, starved, beaten and killed simply for the fact they loved and worshipped God. Atheistic communism hated God and His people and was determined to stamp them out. The author wrote from first hand knowledge. This man had walked, talked and lived with God in prison for 14 long years. I read his book through tears."

That original book is in our archives at the Australian office, and in it Reg has written "This book changed the course of my life".

Many lives have changed course because of *Tortured for Christ* and still today it impacts those who read it.

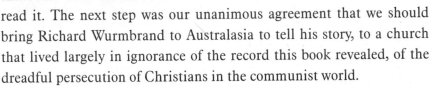

I am one of several friends to whom Reg passed the book with his insistence that we needed to read it. The next step was our unanimous agreement that we should bring Richard Wurmbrand to Australasia to tell his story, to a church that lived largely in ignorance of the record this book revealed, of the dreadful persecution of Christians in the communist world.

In September 1968 a letter of invitation was written by Dr Les Werry, Director of Ambassadors for Christ. Now, on that day almost a year later, we stood in the arrivals hall at Sydney Airport waiting for Richard Wurmbrand to appear.

Suddenly there he was! We had never met him before but there was no mistake. This was Richard Wurmbrand coming to meet us and coming to bring his message from God, from his heart and from his experiences, to Christians in Australia. But would anyone come to hear him?

We were not disappointed. Richard Wurmbrand spoke at meetings across Australia in Sydney, Melbourne, Brisbane, Adelaide and Perth and many regional centres. People came; they came in their thousands. I remember when he spoke at St. Andrew's Cathedral in Sydney during those 1969 meetings. The Cathedral was full and people crowded around the doors and windows to listen.

In those early years – the late sixties and early seventies – similar little dramas were played out in other countries. First in the United States in 1967, and later in South Africa, the United Kingdom, Germany, Switzerland and other countries in Europe. People thronged to hear the message of this living martyr. They came to hear his message of love for the persecutors who, he said, needed to know that God loved them and Jesus Christ died for them.

Richard Wurmbrand had come to the West to be the voice of the martyrs. He had come from behind what was known as the Iron Curtain. Winston Churchill, the wartime Prime Minister of Britain described it in a speech he made in 1946. He said, "From Stettin in the Baltic to Trieste in the Adriatic an iron curtain has descended across the Continent. Behind that line lie all the capitals of the ancient states of Central and Eastern Europe. Warsaw, Berlin, Prague, Vienna, Budapest, Belgrade, Bucharest and Sofia; all these famous cities and the populations around them lie in what I

At the end of his first Australian tour, Pastor Wurmbrand asked us to consider establishing a branch of his new mission in Australia. After a time of discussion and prayer it was decided to set something up as a department of Ambassadors for Christ International, the organisation that invited him to visit this country.

This was done and work began, operating from an office in Blackheath in the Blue Mountains

Blackheath NSW, where VOM-Australia began.

of NSW. Merv Knight was appointed Organising Secretary and published the first Australian newsletter in November 1969. Reg Werry was the Director.

The work grew and in 1972 it was separated from Ambassadors and incorporated as a non-profit organisation in the name of Christian Mission to the Communist World Ltd.

must call the Soviet sphere, and all are subject, in one form or another, not only to Soviet influence but to a very high and in some cases increasing measure of control from Moscow."

It was from here that Richard Wurmbrand came, to tell the world about the suffering and persecution of Christians at the hands of godless, atheistic communists. While he did this, and while he pleaded that we in the West should remember the church in chains, he reminded us that we also needed to love the communists that we might win them, at least some of them, to Christ.

We were privileged to welcome Richard and Sabina Wurmbrand to Australia five more times after the initial 1969 visit, until their last visit in 1981. After this, long distance travel became too difficult for them. Nevertheless it was a joy to join them on many occasions in other parts of the world and to share in numerous facets of the international ministry.

From the messages and the travels of Richard and Sabina Wurmbrand, supported by their son Michael at their office in Glendale, California, Jesus to the Communist World, which in later years would be as Voice of the Martyrs, began its work. In many countries faithful men and women who were called by God, responded to the urgent need to do something, to take action on behalf of their persecuted brothers and sisters.

For the next 29 years the Wurmbrands criss-crossed the world to be a voice for the martyr

Shortly after the fall of the Iron Curtain in 1989 the name was changed to Voice of the Martyrs. This reflected the mission's wider outreach to Christians persecuted under a number of oppressive regimes.

In 1973 the office was moved to Gymea, a suburb of Sydney and three years later to premises a few kilometres away at Sutherland. In 1978 deteriorating health forced co-founder Reg Werry's retirement from active involvement on a day to day basis. He remained on the Board for some years. Merv Knight was appointed Executive Director and the office was moved temporarily to Blaxland in the Lower Blue Mountains, until premises were found in Penrith, where it remained until 2002.

The mission continued to grow and more space was needed. The headquarters of Mission Publications of Australia, located at Lawson in the Blue Mountains, came onto the market at that time. Voice of the Martyrs was able to acquire it and relocate the ministry to this more adequate facility.

In 2005 Merv Knight retired as Executive Director and handed these responsibilities to John Wilson who continues to lead the mission today. Merv continues to serve as Executive Consultant.

church – Scandinavia, North America, Britain, Europe, Australia, New Zealand, India, South Africa to name a few countries where he ministered. Large crowds in all of these countries felt the impact of this man's message and responded in a remarkable way.

At the same time the mission offices, which had been founded in many countries, worked tirelessly together to clandestinely and with sanctified imagination, bring Bibles, practical help and a sense of fellowship within the body of Christ to the persecuted church. Posing as tourists or as businessmen, couriers, both men and women, entered restricted nations to make contact with believers in the underground church.

In this brief summary of the work begun by Richard Wurmbrand it is not meant to list everyone who played a role. It would be a long list. One or two people who made a remarkable contribution should be mentioned. The mission in Germany was led by Hans Braun for 30 years. His leadership was visionary and innovative and much of the work today bears his

Hans Braun.

Hedi Fluri.

footprint. In Switzerland dedicated leadership of the mission's thrust into Africa was given by Sr Hedi Fluri. Some of our significant ministry in Africa today is built on the foundation she laid. She also played an important role for many years in setting up operations to smuggle Bibles, money, and other kinds of help into the communist world. Hedi did a superb job for more than 30 years. She went to be with the Lord on 8 September 2006.

In 1989 we witnessed the revolution in Romania and other parts of Eastern Europe. Soon the Berlin Wall came down and the Iron Curtain crumbled. Varying degrees of religious liberty now exist in countries that previously had their prisons full of believers. The borders of Romania opened and within days a small convoy of vehicles, arranged by our German mission, delivered Bibles and aid to our brothers and sisters.

When the group arrived in Romania their vehicles were suddenly surrounded by armed soldiers. The officer jumped from his patrol car, demanding to know what they were doing there. As he confronted the leader of our team he noticed a Bible through the window of one of the cars and quickly asked,

Christmas 1989 VOM takes aid to Romania.

"Are you Christians?" When our leader answered in the affirmative the officer embraced him and said, "I am a Christian too, welcome to Romania". He then instructed the soldiers to help unload the trucks and distribute the aid.

Within a couple of months of the collapse of the Iron Curtain I was able to travel by car with Hans Braun and Hedi Fluri into Romania. We went to assess the situation for ourselves and take part in planning the mission's first steps to establish VOM ministry in our founder's homeland.

The Soviet Union collapsed and the Commonwealth of Independent States (CIS) was established. At that time Voice of the Martyrs (VOM) workers started evangelistic ministry in co-operation with pastors from the CIS. Ten tonnes of Christian literature, Bibles and other books, were distributed during the first trip in the early 90s shortly after the borders opened. Great shipments followed over the years.

Far from signalling the end of the ministry of VOM, the collapse of the Soviet Union presented opportunities to do more than ever before. We soon discovered that it was one thing to remove the people from communism, but something else to remove communism from the people. Suitable Christian literature became a high priority.

The Commonwealth of Independent States and the countries of Eastern Europe were desperately poor and everything was worn out and dilapidated. Christians in these countries recognised the opportunity to evangelize – to reach their people for Christ. But they had nothing.

VOM worked openly with pastors who previously worked underground, to use this period of time to the best advantage. Even now, nobody knows how long this openness for Christian witness will last – we must redeem the time! Ephesians 5:16. As we look across this area of the world in 2009 we see many signs of continuing repression throughout large parts of what was once the Soviet empire. Some of it bears the hallmark of communism; in other areas it is Islam at work; and elsewhere other forces opposed to the freedom of people to worship God make their presence felt.

After 25 years' exile, Richard Wurmbrand returns to Romania.

In 1990, at 81 years-of-age, Pastor and Mrs Wurmbrand ended 25 years of exile from their homeland and returned to Romania for preaching engagements. During this visit they officially opened the Stephanus Christian Bookshop established in Bucharest by VOM.

In September 1991 they visited Russia for ministry, in association with Pastor Josef Bondarenko who was one of the organisers of our first evangelistic trips. As a young man of 22, Josef Bondarenko was jailed by the KGB for the "crime" of preaching. He was jailed three times and altogether served ten-and-a-half years in prison. During his first jail sentence Bondarenko led an infamous thief and killer to the Lord. During his last term in jail Josef led a KGB colonel to the Lord.

During the 90s the activities of VOM continued to grow. A Christian centre – "Stephanus" – was opened in Moscow. This became a distribution point for Christian literature and practical aid. Bible study groups were coordinated through Stephanus until 1998 when, because of changing circumstances and the growth of the local church, the centre was closed.

An office was also opened in Ukraine at Cherkassy, where a Russian language newsletter was produced and thousands of Christian books distributed.

In Romania in the 90s a printing plant was developed together with the Stephanus bookshop in Bucharest and a few years later, the Agape Children's Home was opened at Pascani in north-eastern Romania. The printing plant was closed after about 10 years when commercial plants had been established where material could be produced more economically.

Printing press installed in Romania.

Albania, "the first atheist state", saw the demise of communism in the mid-90s. In the capital Tirana, "The Stephen Center" – providing a coffee shop, Christian book shop and meeting facilities – was run with help from VOM, until it became strong enough to operate independently.

At the same time the continuing communist world has not been forgotten and much activity is supported in places such as Vietnam, Laos, North Korea, Cuba and China.

RICHARD WURMBRAND

Pastor Wurmbrand has been called "a modern apostle Paul". At the time of St. Paul's conversion, God said, "he is a chosen vessel unto Me, to bear My Name before the Gentiles, and kings, and the children of Israel, for I will show him how great things he must suffer for My Name's sake" (Acts 9:15,16). Richard Wurmbrand could have had little inkling of what he was to suffer for the cause of Christ. The village carpenter, who led Wurmbrand to Christ, had no idea of the future that lay before the new convert and what a great work God had chosen him to do.

Somewhere I read this statement: "Every person's life intersects history – only a few impact it". Richard Wurmbrand's life is one that has impacted history.

All outstanding characters in history, religious as well as political, have been criticised. A leader with strong convictions and forthrightness, of necessity has his enemies and opponents. The footsteps of Christ Himself were dogged by His antagonists, laying traps for Him, trying to catch Him off guard, twisting His words, and stirring up popular opinion against Him. The religious leaders were His worst foes.

Richard Wurmbrand, as a servant of God, came in for a good measure of criticism, but he was able to persevere. He never wanted the harsh things kept from him; he accepted the bad with the good. He was always willing to reply to questions and defend his statements. In fact, it was his firm belief that, given the opportunity, he could often win over his opponents and turn his critics into friends.

He was large-hearted enough to forgive; not too difficult for one who, with absolute sincerity and truthfulness, claimed to love his jailers and torturers.

His three-fold ministry was to resist atheistic communism, to assist the underground church and to win communists for Christ. He had no self-interests. He put amazing energy and hours of time, day and night, into this task. Nothing made him happier than to know that help was reaching Christian prisoners, their families and pastors and believers who were persecuted for their faith, and that the good news of God's love and grace was being spread throughout the world. As world events unfolded, he displayed the same passion to work in the Muslim world.

Preaching, writing, travelling, pleading, praying – often to the point of utter exhaustion – there is no doubt that Richard Wurmbrand and his wife were wholeheartedly dedicated to God and His work.

Richard Wurmbrand was accused of exaggerating his experiences; it has been rather the reverse. We have been told independently by someone who spent some years in prison with Pastor Wurmbrand that "he has not told everything. If he did, no one in the West would believe it".

Consider the case of Josef Bondarenko who was so helpful when the Wurmbrands first visited Russia in 1991. In 1966 it was reported in the press that five leaders of "dissident" Russian Baptists were sentenced to jail by a court in Kiev. Moscow radio said the defendants were also charged with conducting illegal Sunday schools for children aged five to fourteen years, and organising gatherings of fellow-believers in the countryside around Kiev.

Josef Bondarenko

One of these leaders was Josef Bondarenko, long ago released after completing his prison sentences. He sent telegrams to all his faithful prayer supporters, thanking them for their help through the years. He was imprisoned several times. In prison God used his witness for the salvation of other prisoners. He testified that his punishment was that he had to stand knee deep in water for a month, with no light and no bed. He was told that the water was punishment for kneeling to pray.

There was also the arrest of Khamara of Kulunda which was reported in the press. He died under tortures in prison. His corpse was returned to his family to frighten them and other believers into submission. On his

Nicolai Khamara.

body were the marks of his suffering – burns, wounds and bruises from beating and stabbing. And this was not all. His tongue had been cut out and his mouth stuffed with cotton wool.

From these horrible sufferings Khamara, too, was released, passing into the glorious presence of his Saviour and into the joy of his Lord. When the picture of this martyr was shown, the vast audience at the Royal Festival Hall in London stood to honour the memory of one who was faithful unto death.

Nikolai Khamara was arrested for robbery and imprisoned for ten years. Khamara watched the Christians and wondered what kind of beings they were. They were men, but they would show joy despite their suffering and would sing in very dark hours. When they had a piece of bread, they shared it with someone who had none. Their faces would shine as they spoke to someone whom Khamara could not see.

One day two Christians sat down with Khamara and asked him about his story. Khamara told them his sad tale and finished by saying, "I am a lost man".

One of the Christians, with a smile, asked Khamara, "If somebody loses a gold ring, what is the value of that gold ring when it is lost?"

"What a foolish question! A gold ring is a gold ring. You have lost it, but somebody else will have it." "A very good answer," said the Christian. "Now tell me, what is the value of a lost man? A lost man, even a thief, an adulterer, or a murderer, has the whole value of a man.

He is of such value that the Son of God forsook heaven for him and died on the cross to save him."

The Christian said to the robber, "You may have been lost, but God's love can find you." Hearing this, Khamara gave his life to Christ.

A letter was received from the underground church in Romania before the 1989 revolution, and we quote, "Many have asked us about the situation here. I have read the books by Brother Wurmbrand and can tell only that the things which he writes and says are no exaggerations but pure reality . . ."

On handbills prepared for a special meeting at the Royal Festival Hall in London, arranged by his publishers, Hodder & Stoughton, Richard Wurmbrand was announced as "one of the most remarkable figures of the twentieth century."

It gives a little insight into the heart of the man when we read his comment on this statement:

"It is not easy to bear what is written on the invitations. I wonder by what I am one of the most remarkable figures of the century? Poor century! What about Einstein, or the missionaries eaten in the Congo? When St. Ignatius was taken from Smyrna to Rome to be thrown to the wild beasts, brethren everywhere kissed his chains. He was horrified and said, 'You will make me lose the sense of the death I have to endure'. Princess Ileana, a member of the Romanian royal family, when she was converted could not bear it any more to be called 'Royal Highness'. But she bore it as being useful for Christian work. Let us take it like this, and may God keep us all humble."

CONVERSION AND EARLY MINISTRY

———————— ⟨⟩ ————————

Richard Wurmbrand, the youngest of four sons of a dentist, was born into a poor Jewish home in Bucharest, Romania. As a child of nine he was orphaned when his father died and knew what it was to hunger for bread as well as for love and security. He grew up calling himself an atheist and a Marxist.

As he worked, bettering his position and earning more money, he lived for the pleasures of sin, gratifying every selfish lust. But his life as a sophisticated playboy did not bring him the satisfaction he had longed for as a poor orphan.

Mr and Mrs C Wölfkes.

It was 1937, and in one of the many mountain villages in Romania lived Mr Christian Wölfkes, a godly old German carpenter. He had a fervent love for the Jews and desired above all else that before he died he would be able to win a Jew for Christ. But there were no Jews in his village, and he was ill and had no strength or money to travel in search of any Jew to whom he could testify. He asked God to send a Jew to him, and in a wonderful way God answered his prayer.

Suffering from tuberculosis and advised by his doctor to rest in the mountains, Richard Wurmbrand and his wife arrived in the village.

There, for the first time in their lives, the embittered atheists encountered a man who simply lavished love and kindness upon them. For hours the old carpenter prayed for these Jewish strangers and sought by all means possible to lead them to the Saviour.

Auschwitz.

Love triumphed; Richard and Sabina Wurmbrand were truly converted.

Before long they knew what it meant to suffer for Christ's sake. During the Nazi terror they were repeatedly beaten and arrested. Mrs. Wurmbrand's family perished in the mass extermination of Jews.

We know there are Christians in every nation who demonstrate the courage and grace of Christ in spite of the obstacles they face. Sabina Wurmbrand, was such a witness.

Her Jewish family was killed by the Nazis. She and her husband were imprisoned by the Communists. Nevertheless, Sabina always thought of others and their needs. When Russian soldiers were taking over Bulgaria after invading her homeland of Romania, Sabina, carrying Bibles and bags of salt, climbed onto the roof of a Russian troop train heading into Bulgaria.

Sketch of Sabina riding on the roof of a train on the way to Bulgaria.

The salt was for persecuted Bulgarian Christians to sell to feed their families. The invading soldiers were seated down below, but the spiritual invasion was on the roof. It was this spirit that would enable the Wurmbrands to survive the years of prison and deprivation under communism, and later to found the ministry of VOM.

As the situation in Romania worsened and people began to taste starvation, Richard Wurmbrand obtained from Christians abroad just a few thousand dollars. Americans sent also packages with food but they were to a large extent not Romanian staple foods and unsophisticated Romanians, even children, did not know what to make of M&M candies, Hershey chocolate bars or even powdered milk, avocado, etc.

Richard, before his conversion, had been a stockbroker. So also had been a close cousin of his by marriage, named Saiovici. Saiovici also became a Christian.

As it happened, there was some exceptional situation in 1946 where a financial investment offered the possibility of an outstanding yield. Richard Wurmbrand and Saiovici invested $3,000-$4,000 in this situation in which they felt they were professionals. Within two or three weeks it was transformed into over $100,000 and for that time in Romania, converted into the local currency, Richard became a multimillionaire.

Thus, together with Saiovici and the Norwegian mission to the Jews he made the communists very upset by purchasing whole railroad cars of wheat. He organised a public kitchen where about 1000 people could get at least one meal a day. The kitchen functioned for something like seven or eight months.

Richard also organised two summer camps where, with some of the same money, he paid for about 250 or 300 clergy, of all denominations, to spend two to three weeks of vacation in a mountain resort named Predeal. Here he explained to them the ABC of what a communist takeover would mean for the church and Christian witness.

Br Saiovici is seen here, fourth from left in front row at one of the Predeal meetings.

HIS WORK UNDER COMMUNISM

Since the first day of his conversion, Richard had a burning desire to win atheists and Russians for Christ. In 1944 the communists seized power in Romania and a million Russian troops poured into the country. With his knowledge of Russian, as well as several other languages, opportunities abounded to preach the Gospel. Wurmbrand engaged in a two-fold ministry – to his own oppressed countrymen and to the Russians. He boarded trains and used the long journeys to preach the Gospel; in disguise he went into Russian army camps and expounded the Word of God with Christian soldiers "on guard".

Many would never have attempted to carry on a Christian ministry in such conditions as were imposed upon Romania during the Soviet occupation. With amazing ingenuity Wurmbrand pursued his missionary activities among the Russians and led the "underground" church for a number of years. Souls were saved and the church grew. Thousands of Gospels were printed on secret presses in a format which passed the communist censors. So effective was the work of Richard Wurmbrand and his devoted colleagues that he was arrested

Secret printing press.

and imprisoned by the Secret Police in 1948. His wife was arrested in 1950.

On 29 February 1948, a beautiful Sunday morning, Richard Wurmbrand set out on foot for his church in Bucharest. He never arrived.

Wurmbrand's disappearance was expected. Anyone who acted contrary to the regime could expect imprisonment or death. At a "Congress of Cults" held by the Communist government, religious leaders stepped forward to swear loyalty to the new regime. Sabina whispered to Richard he should "wipe the shame from the face of Jesus". Richard replied that if he did this, she would no longer have a husband. "I don't need a coward for a husband," she answered. So Richard stepped forward and told the 4000 delegates that their duty as Christians was to glorify God and Christ alone.

What had actually happened on that Sunday morning in 1948? As Richard walked to church, a van of the secret police stopped in front of him. Four men jumped out and hustled him inside. He was taken to their headquarters and later locked in a solitary cell where he was designated Prisoner Number One.

His years of imprisonment consisted of a ceaseless round of torture and brainwashing. For seventeen hours a day he heard phrases repeated over and over: Communism is good. Christianity is stupid! Nobody loves you any more! Give up. Give up! Over the years, his body was burned with red-hot pokers, and carved in a dozen places. "I prefer not to speak about those times through which I have passed," he said. "When I do, I cannot sleep at night. It is too painful." While torturing him, his jailers also broke many of his bones, including four vertebrae. Miraculously, he survived. Later Richard told us he discovered the antidote to brainwashing was heartwashing – having a heart cleansed by the love of Christ.

More than eight years later, in 1956, Wurmbrand was released. Sabina herself was brutalized for three years in prison and labour camp.

She was put to work as a slave labourer to take part in building the Danube Canal. The canal was designed to connect the North Sea and the Black Sea and was eventually finished in 1992. Mihai (Michael), the 11-year-old son of the Wurmbrands, was orphaned during this time.

The police first made an inventory of everything in the Wurmbrand home, then locked the flat and left 11-year-old Mihai in the street. Later, practically everything in the flat was confiscated.

In 1990 Sabina visits unfinished Danube Canal.

At this time, a long-time friend and co-worker of the Wurmbrand family, Alice Panaiodor, rescued Mihai from the street and took him and Radu, an orphaned boy who had been living with the Wurmbrand family, to stay with her. In her book, *Walk Through Flames* she said, "We were crowded, and we were poor, but God took care of us. In a miraculous way I was able not only to feed the children but to send food parcels to Sabina, and even to help other families who had relatives in prison. Many Christians contributed gifts from their own meagre supplies." Mihai lived with Alice until his mother was released from prison in 1953. In 1959 Alice Panaiodor was arrested.

Released, the Wurmbrands immediately recommenced secret church work.

Wurmbrand was arrested again and returned to prison. He was not released until 1964. He told us, "the last words my wife said to me in the presence of the police before they took me away were, 'Richard, you shall be brought before governors for My sake, for a testimony to the gentiles' Matthew 10:18. And so it happened. A member of the cabinet, General Negrea, questioned me. He had even read a book of mine. I could tell him about Jesus."

In 1965 churches in Scandinavia ransomed Wurmbrand from Romania for $US10,000. Richard and Sabina immediately spoke out for those still suffering at the hands of communists. Wurmbrand was invited to testify before a U.S. Senate committee.

When it was his turn to speak, Richard Wurmbrand was impatient to begin and the chairman of the committee asked him to wait. We see that Pastor Wurmbrand was not ready to wait when we read a part of his testimony, as recorded in the Congressional Record:

"'No, I will not wait! I have waited fourteen years in prison. When you ate coconut pies, we have eaten excrement and urine. Only I have to decide. Not you! I speak in the name of one billion enslaved men! I have not feared the Nazis ... I have not feared the communists ... I have spoken. And I will speak here even if the Court will rule otherwise!'

"With these defiant words, Rev Richard Wurmbrand, who had been imprisoned in Romania for 14 years for his religious activities, removed his tunic to show the scars on his chest and back resulting from communist tortures. He showed the Senators eighteen holes cut in his body.

"'I don't care about what anybody objects. He should object against what is happening in America – this collusion and this apathy towards those who torture Christians,' the minister shouted. The audience burst into applause and a standing ovation. A Lithuanian reporter who had escaped her homeland cried. The defence respectfully sat silent as Rev Wurmbrand continued his testimony of religious persecution, torture and terror under the communists in Romania. The evangelical minister, who was released from prison in 1964, told the Court:

"'Nobody on earth is in prison without being tortured in the most horrible manner. Within the prison . . . Christians have been tied to crosses for days, for nights. The crosses were put on the floor every night and other prisoners were beaten and tortured to fulfil their bodily necessities upon the faces and bodies of the saints of God. And then the crosses were erected again and the guards stood around, jeering, mocking, "Look your Christ! How beautiful he is. What fragrances he brings from Heaven!"'

"The minister testified that Westerners were being deceived about a so-called revival of religious activities in communist countries as personified by the Baptist Church in Moscow. He said that Moscow is a town of seven million inhabitants and that for these seven million inhabitants there is only this one church, which is not solely for Baptists but for all Protestants.

"Before his testimony concluded, Rev Wurmbrand rhetorically asked why is it necessary to have underground churches, which he said are flourishing, if there is religious freedom under the communists. He reiterated to the Court – 'Never has there been such anti-religious persecution as there is today'."

In the years to follow he was invited to speak before hundreds of groups in many places around the world.

By 1967, "Prisoner Number One" had incorporated the mission organisation that is now known as Voice of the Martyrs, dedicated to assisting those throughout the world who are persecuted for their active faith in Christ.

Richard and Sabina were able to survive their ordeal through the power of love. "If the heart is cleansed by the love of Jesus Christ," wrote Wurmbrand, "and if the heart loves him, you can resist all tortures. What would a loving bride not do for a loving bridegroom? What would a loving mother not do for her child? If you love Christ as Mary did, who had Christ as a baby in her arms, if you love Jesus as a bride loves her bridegroom, then you can resist such tortures. God will judge us not according to how much we endured, but how much we could love. I am a witness for the Christians in communist prisons that they could love. They could love God and men."

Life in the prisons of communist Romania defies description. The story of Wurmbrand's imprisonment has been recounted in his books. Through his tale of horror shines the glory of God's faithfulness and the triumph of His grace. Wurmbrand's testimony bears the hallmark of truth and it is the reality of his spiritual experiences that has touched the hearts of thousands of his readers, and challenged them to a deeper love for Christ. It was during his time in solitary confinement, sentenced to 25 years, ill and with little hope of release that Richard dreamed he would be set free and would start a mission to proclaim Jesus to the communists, and that he would open a Christian book shop in Romania. This was his dream and his prayer.

In later years he encouraged people in his meetings to dream of great things, impossible things they could do for God, to pray about them and trust God to bring them to pass.

50 YEARS A SMUGGLER

Whistles sounded and dogs barked.

The border guards rushed to join the officer who was waving his arms. With the Second World War over and the map of Europe redrawn, the Soviet troops were zealously guarding the borders and checking every suspicious event. There was tension on the border with Romania and the guards were constantly on the alert to prevent Soviet citizens escaping to Eastern Europe.

As the guards clustered around their officer, he was shouting and pointing to four sets of footprints in the snow. Obviously they had been made recently under cover of darkness and were clearly heading across no-man's land towards Romania. The group of guards scanned the horizon but knew a search would be fruitless because the fugitives were long gone. They could only hope they would be picked up by the Romanian police.

In a cold attic apartment in Romania, two weary but triumphant Christians were talking with Pastor Richard Wurmbrand. They told him how they had followed his advice. They had walked backwards in the snow when they crossed the border into the Soviet Union to safely deliver precious Bibles to their brethren in the underground church. Then on their return they walked directly across the border back to Romania. They laughed a little as they imagined the frustrated Russian border guards enraged at another four citizens who had "escaped to

Romania". This was the beginning of the smuggling work that would continue for many decades.

Each year on 23 August the 1944 sellout of Romania was commemorated as the day Romania was "liberated". Russian troops poured into the country. These were Romania's new "allies". It was thus that Romania, which had been known as the granary of Europe, became a starvation area as Russia stole machinery and anything else of value and carried it back across the border.

Pastor Wurmbrand said, "I speak good Russian. It was easy for me to talk to Russian soldiers in streets, shops, and on trains. I did not wear clerical dress, so they thought I was an ordinary citizen. The younger men especially were bewildered and homesick.

"They were pleased to be shown the sights of Bucharest and to be invited to a friendly home. I had help from many young Christians who spoke Russian. I told the girls they could use their beauty to help bring men to Christ. One girl saw a soldier and suggested they go somewhere for a talk. 'With you, anywhere!' said the Russian, and she brought him to my house. The soldier was converted, and brought others to us.

"We secretly published the Gospel in Russian. Over the next three years about a million books were distributed in cafes, parks, railway stations – wherever Russians were to be found. They were passed from hand to hand until they fell to pieces. Many of our helpers were arrested, but none gave me away."

Bianca Adler.

One of Richard Wurmbrand's workers in those days was a young woman known now as Bianca Adler. Bianca was converted under Richard's ministry before he went to prison.

Mrs Adler tells the story: "When the Soviets came to Romania, a million soldiers including officers and the KGB, with guns and everything, arrived in the country.

"They spread lots of terror in the population, first of all because they were very wild Soviet soldiers. They would go to hotels and even to the pharmacies and drink any kind of spirit they could find. They got drunk and not only stole a lot but also did a lot of killing. If anyone refused to give them everything they wanted, the soldiers simply killed them.

"The local authority had given a written order that no girls or women were to be on the street after nine o'clock at night, even though it was summer and it was still light at that time. The order was given because many women, especially young women and girls, were found in the morning raped and killed, with their throats slashed by the Soviets. There was such terror in the country. The government even 'exported' a lot of people to Russia.

"The first day the Russians entered Romania, Richard and Sabina Wurmbrand were on the main railway station of Bucharest to meet them and see what kind of people they were.

"They met the people who came in the first tank – two young Soviet officers. The officers asked, 'What can you offer us now? We are the victors'. Sabina offered them a Russian Bible and said, 'This is the most precious gift that I can offer you'. So one officer took the Bible, and said, 'Why do we need the Bible? Tell us better where we can find Vodka, something to drink!' Then the other one said, 'but thank you anyway' and took the Bible with him.

"Richard and Sabina came home and the Lord started to speak to their hearts. 'What are we going to do with these people?' they thought. 'There must be a reason that the Lord has permitted them to invade our country. The communists, since the Russian revolution, have kept so many people under the darkness of atheism, of Marxism-Leninism. Atheism says that there is no God, and children are taught from kindergarten to the grave that there is no God. All this religious doctrine is pumped into people by force and by compulsion. But we are Christians and have the Bible, and we know that they are precious souls for whom Christ has died. And they have to be saved too. But how do we do that?'

"Richard told Sabina, 'You remember very well that I was an atheist, and so were you. So many times I have prayed, now that I have become a Christian, and asked the Lord to show me how to tell the people that God exists and that Christ is His Son and our Saviour'.

"When they were praying about the way, the Lord showed Richard a small printer in a back street, a Jewish man. Although the man worked at great risk for himself – Richard probably paid him extra to take the risk – he started to print small Gospels in the Russian language. I think it was the Gospel of John.

"Richard took aside several of us young people – I was then twenty-one or twenty-two – and some other friends, and told us what was happening. He said that it was not coincidence; nothing that the Lord permits in our lives or in the life of a nation is a coincidence.

"'The fact is that the Lord permitted these people to come to our country, not knowing anything about the richness that is in Christ and salvation, and made us missionaries and me a preacher. We know that the Gospel is to be preached to every creature.

"'The Lord has shown us a way, but we need several people to go to the various railway stations in Bucharest by which the Soviet troops are coming home or going back to the front,' Richard said. All the time there was traffic like that, thousands of soldiers on the move. There were no trains for the people because only the Soviet soldiers used them.

"Richard asked us, 'Who among you would be ready to take the risk? You should know from the beginning that there is a great risk – you may be imprisoned, sent to Siberia, or even killed. But are you ready to do all this for Christ or not? Has Christ done enough for you so that you will take this thing upon yourselves, being ready at least to pay the price even if this means death?'

"Richard spoke to us very convincingly, not that we were great heroes, and I was the least hero of all. I was very frightened. I believe that he must have prayed very earnestly with Sabina for this special meeting with us. Several of us then went to the main railway station. I took a large bag containing hundreds of Gospels.

"We knew that the KGB – their guardians, as we would call them – were in the train. So Richard told us what would be the best way for us to work.

"We went alone or in pairs. The trains were very, very long and I was almost at the last car, with my bag of Russian gospels. I waited like one of the people who were looking at the soldiers. We knew that the only KGB man was in the front near the locomotive, usually near the conductor, so we stood by the last car.

"When the train started to move, we began throwing all those hundreds of Gospels through the windows to the soldiers. By the time the KGB man in front, maybe twenty, thirty, or forty cars away, found out what we were doing, the train was already far away. From that distance we could hear the KGB man curse us in Russian – all kinds of things. I didn't know much Russian, but I understood the curses because so many of the soldiers used them. Oh, he cursed us so!

"As the train rolled by, the soldiers quickly caught the Gospels and hid them in their uniforms. Then they moved through the train cars and mixed with the others. More soldiers came and stood in their place. When the KGB man came to the last car, he could not find them. This was one method. We continued this until Richard's arrest." Bianca's story can be found in her book *Serving God in Hostile Territory*, available from VOM.

Although he passed away in 2001, for those who follow him Pastor Wurmbrand continues to be an inspiration to take the message of love and hope to restricted nations, and to bring help and comfort to His persecuted church. Richard never let borders hinder his determination. Neither should we!

THE VOICE OF THE UNDERGROUND CHURCH

There is no doubt that the members of Pastor Wurmbrand's congregation and many others in Romania held him in high esteem and love. When he was still in prison and had been reported dead, one of the members of his church went day after day to the prisons, tirelessly searching, for she knew within her spirit that he was alive.

In a miraculous way, God worked and gave her the evidence that he was indeed living. I, with many of our workers, came to know this dear sister in later years in the person of Bianca Adler. Some of her story is recounted in the previous chapter.

A rumour was heard in Bucharest that relatives of someone who was missing could present themselves twice a week at a certain office in Calea Rahovei where information would be given. Sabina asked Bianca to go there on behalf of "her brother" Richard.

Bianca told me she went and waited in line for her turn to enter. As she waited she was whispering to the lady next to her. Bianca was facing into the courtyard while the other lady was facing toward the building. Suddenly the lady drew her attention to one of the small basement windows at ground level and whispered to her, "be careful not to be observed, but it seems that a man is at the window and is pointing at you as if he wants to give some message to you." Bianca slowly turned and looked. Surely there was the face of a man. He was very thin, like a skeleton, unshaved and with blackened eyes. The sunlight in the courtyard was very bright and she blinked her eyes. Then, she was sure. Yes, it was him. Richard was alive! So Bianca was the one who brought the message to Sabina that, indeed, her husband was alive.

With the passing of time Bianca and her husband Dr Tom Adler took up leadership of VOM in New Zealand. When Tom died unexpectedly in 1983 after three years in New Zealand, Bianca continued the work alone until she retired in 1999.

In 1972 I had the privilege to meet another member of Pastor Wurmbrand's

Bianca Adler in New Zealand.

church, who had been able to leave Romania before his arrest by the communists. She worked for years to obtain the release of Richard and Sabina Wurmbrand. Anutza Moise, who went to live in Norway until the Lord called her home, recorded the story in her book, *One of God's Smallest*. It is another chapter in the life of VOM. Anutza tells of an experience during the Second World War. It was 1944 and the people were accustomed to using air raid shelters. On one occasion, the air raid warning had ended but several hours passed and Richard had not come home. They feared he might have been arrested.

Anutza said, "I went to their home to see if they were all right and found Sabina, who had stayed in the flat that day, so ill with worry she could scarcely stand. As our anxiety increased, we went out in search of him, only to be met at one police station after another with the same answer: 'He is not here'. I had to lead Sabina back by the hand, she was so weak. Finally we gave up and went home. As we opened the door, Richard got up from a chair. 'Where on earth have you been?' he asked. 'I was getting worried.' Sabina nearly fainted. 'Where have you been,' I countered. 'We've been looking for you all over Bucharest.' 'Oh' said Richard cheerfully, 'I've been having a wonderful time.' And he proceeded to tell us what a marvellous opportunity he had had to witness for Christ to the police who had arrested him.

"Poor Sabina! It was a good thing she did not know then what life had in store for her. Better still! She knew she had a wonderful Saviour, who was to prove His power in His faithful servants during the critical times through which they were to live."

Anutza was able to escape to Norway in 1947. She tells that not long after her arrival she received a short note from Sabina, saying, "Richard is ill in the sanatorium" from which she knew that he was in prison again. She said, "My heart went out to her, knowing well how much they would have to suffer. I knew, probably better than anyone else, how much she adored Richard, and how he depended on her. But she would never show her despair."

Anutza Moise.

Anutza told us, "Richard and Sabina were and are my closest friends on earth. I had tried hard to persuade them to come with me when I was leaving, but they refused.

"We found out later that Richard had been given an earlier opportunity to flee the country, for he knew only too well what to expect from the current regime. The Swedish Ambassador in Romania offered generously to help him in this by sending the embassy car that had diplomatic immunity to whisk him and his family out of the country at night. He would have done so but a very unusual warning came to him from the Lord, via a Christian lady who seemed to have the gift of prophecy. This happened during a night of vigil and prayer. Such all-night meetings were often held in the Wurmbrand house. She uttered the following message, 'You shepherd who wish to leave your flock, know this: a true shepherd will never abandon his sheep, but stays with them whatever happens. . .' Richard and Sabina believed God still had work for them to do in Romania and they stayed.

"After this they passed through unspeakable hardships in prisons and labour camps – Richard for a total of 14 years. Something of how that experience had marked him was revealed in a strange and remarkable letter he wrote to me a few weeks after his release.

"Some of Richard's comments were: 'I am slowly getting used to my new circumstances of life. I am finding, too, that one's spiritual life takes on new aspects when one is back in family life. Separated from my family and from the brethren, I was enfolded in divine embraces . . . Quietly, without even asking a single question, I simply rested . . . While in the world of the Spirit, which I have been inhabiting up to the present . . . everything that happened took place only in my inner self. And the beauties and joys were always pure . . . Now I no longer have this privilege. Sin watches over every step you make, even when you are doing good, even when you are fulfilling God's law. Here you can live only through grace, only by trusting God's compassion and wisdom, which will solve all problems. The law of God gives us a guilty conscience, an unquiet heart, a heart that trembles because of the sins which the law discloses to us without being able to remove them from us. Without it, we live in quiet trust that God is guiding our steps through the maze of our lives – even when things happen to us or we are doing things which we ourselves do not understand'."

I have often reflected on the decision of Pastor and Mrs Wurmbrand to abandon the possibility to flee the country and find safety and comfort elsewhere. It was out of the crucible of suffering to follow that Voice of the Martyrs was born.

Missionaries from the Middle East who visited Eastern Europe not long after the Wurmbrands were ransomed to the West, wrote, "In Romania the believers are more closely watched than elsewhere, but we were asked eager questions. 'How is Richard Wurmbrand and his dear wife who helped us so much?'"

Although imprisonment for Christ was not as common in Romania in later years after the Wurmbrands escaped, it continued until the revolution in 1989 that overthrew Ceausescu and ushered in a measure of freedom. This situation has changed with the passing years, but much remains to be done in other restricted nations where Christians languish in prison, even as we now walk in the twenty-first century.

While visiting Israel, the Director of an American missionary organisation met a man who was in prison in Romania at the same time as Pastor Wurmbrand. This brother told the mission leader, "I was in the same prisons as Wurmbrand for twelve years. What he has said is only ten percent of the truth. He could not say any more . . ."

In the earlier days of VOM we received the following letter concerning the underground church: "Greetings in His precious Name. Enclosed please find a further love gift for the believers in communist Europe. Four friends of ours who visited Czechoslovakia, Hungary and Romania, taking scriptures and other supplies, were able to make contact with many members of the underground church. They were disappointed to find that many leaders of the recognised churches had lost their power and usefulness through compromise with the authorities. How greatly they need our constant prayers and support."

A courier who visited Romania reported a conversation with one of the leaders of the underground church: "Through Richard's books, things are improving. . ."

The couriers brought many letters of love and appreciation for our work from key people in Romanian Christian life. There was one critical voice, warning that our activity might do more harm to the brethren, but there exists no report with concrete facts that anybody has suffered because of this activity.

A letter from an outstanding Lutheran pastor in Romania said, "I read two of your books. I am deeply moved by them. Very often tears came into my eyes. We are all backing you. May God bless your work!"

A personality of the Protestant church in Romania succeeded in emigrating to the West. He wrote, "I read the books published by you, which are full of truth. I appreciated them because they give light in these things, hidden in the kingdom of lies. We also have been persecuted because we are Christians . . ."

In 1969, a letter was smuggled out of the Soviet Union. It was signed by fourteen members of a small congregation in a village underground church. The words are pathetic: "They take away from us the bit of bread, our property, our houses. They deprive us of everything – except eternal love, which has been given to us as a gift by our heavenly Father.

Nobody can deprive us of this. From 23 to 29 June (1969) we will stay fasting. We appeal to all our brethren to call upon the Lord in prayer and fasting that we might remain faithful to Him. We will also pray for our persecutors that God may forgive them and lead them to repentance."

Such fasting and prayer is still a hallmark of the underground church, decades later.

PRAISE AND BLAME

There appeared in Romania from time to time leaflets issued by a political resistance movement. Some of these leaflets praised Pastor Wurmbrand, calling him a hero who distinguished himself in the fight against communism. They called him an eminent representative of an enslaved nation. But they also had a criticism to make.

"The Protestant pastor, Richard Wurmbrand, has given powerful blows to the communist regime by the revelations he has made about the prisons in Romania and about the persecutions to which the church is submitted. Where Pastor Wurmbrand is wrong is in the solutions which he has for fighting against communism and for solving the tragedy of enslaved peoples. After his vehement speeches – he demands forgiveness for the hangmen, hoping for their conversion to Christianity."

The resistance writer went on to say, "Forgiveness can come only after the captive nations have been freed . . . Mr Wurmbrand has to convince those responsible in politics in the West of the necessity of a diplomatic, economic, moral and scientific blockade of the communist world – not relationships with tyrants but the complete severance of all relationships. This remedy is infallible."

However, Pastor Wurmbrand had seen his "remedy" work in wonderful ways. He said that he had many joyful experiences in prison, the greatest being when communist guards were converted.

COMMUNISTS WON FOR CHRIST

Richard told of one officer of the Secret Police who interrogated him, and was in turn "interrogated" by the prisoner about the state of his soul. He repented of his sins and performed great services for Wurmbrand and other Christian prisoners. Eventually he was discovered and imprisoned. It is very difficult to conceal a true conversion.

The first day after he was freed, the ex-police officer came to give Wurmbrand some beautiful flowers saying, "This is a token of my gratitude. You have given me the opportunity of suffering for the cause of Christ. I am thankful."

Pastor Wurmbrand told the story of another conversion:

"One day Lieutenant X summoned me for an interrogation. He had a rubber truncheon in his hand and shouted, 'Here's some paper, write a declaration that you have broken prison rules, and put down the names and all the particulars of everyone you have seen breaking the rules. Write down everything you have said against the communists and what you have heard others saying against us. Make a list of all the prisoners who criticize us. If not . . .'

"There was no need to tell me what would happen 'if not' because he was waving his truncheon. I understood. 'You have half an hour,' he said, and left the room.

"I am not a courageous man, but at that moment God made me forget that I had any cause to fear. I sat down to write . . .

"I admitted that I had often broken prison rules. I had manufactured knives, needles and chess-pieces. I had communicated through the wall by Morse Code with prisoners in neighbouring cells, teaching them verses from the Bible and giving them the Gospel message. I wrote, 'I do not know the names of those who were on the other side of the wall. I have never spoken against the communists. I am an adversary of communism, but I love the communists. I am a disciple of Christ Who has given us love for our enemies. I pray for their conversion. I understand them and wish them to become my brothers in the faith.

"'As for other men, I can give no declaration about what they have said against the communists, for I am a priest of God and a priest can never be a witness for the prosecution against anybody. My calling is to defend and not to accuse.'

"With this I finished and then waited for the officer to come back and beat me. I had been beaten so many times that once more did not make much difference.

"After about an hour he returned, still holding the rubber truncheon in his hand. In the meantime, he had been beating up other prisoners, as I was told afterwards. He took my 'declaration' and began to read it.

"While he read, he put the truncheon on one side, and when he finished he spoke to me, 'Mr Wurmbrand (he had not called me "Mr" before), how is it that you can love me? I would never love someone who put me in prison and beat me up. How can you fulfil such a commandment of Christ?'

"I answered, 'I am not fulfilling a commandment by loving my enemies; Jesus has given me a new character, the main feature of which is love. Just as only water can flow out of a bottle of water, and only milk out of a bottle of milk, so only love can flow out of a loving heart'.

"For about two hours that day we discussed the relationship between Marxism and Christianity, and I found him to be very intelligent. After this he summoned me every day for about two weeks, each time for an hour or two, in order to learn more about the views of Protestant

Christians. He did not believe me when I told him that the first written work by Karl Marx was a commentary on the Gospel of St John. He checked the reference which I had given and found that I had been correct.

"I told him that in the Foreword to 'Capital' Marx wrote, 'Christianity, especially in its Protestant form, is the ideal religion for the renewal of lives made wretched by sin.' My life had been made wretched by sin, I told him. I had followed the advice of Marx and had become a Protestant Christian. He checked the quotation and found that I was right. Our discussions became more and more interesting.

"One day, wearing the uniform of an officer of the Secret Police, he confessed to me who was dressed as a prisoner. We became brothers. After his conversion he tried to do much good to me and to others. I told nobody what had happened between us, but probably he did. He disappeared from our prison and I never saw him again."

This was not the only guard won to Christ by the witness of Richard Wurmbrand. I remember many years later, after the Wurmbrands had been ransomed from Romania and the Mission had been founded, I was at a conference. Standing in the courtyard outside our German mission office waiting for the meetings to begin, I chatted with Pastor Wurmbrand. At a certain moment he put his hand on my arm and moved away to meet a man who was just stepping from a car. The two men

German mission.

met, greeted each other in Romanian, and embraced warmly. I thought this must be one of Richard's co-workers from the past. I discovered later that the newcomer had been one of the guards in a Romanian prison who had interrogated and beaten Richard Wurmbrand. Love had won and the man had converted to Christ and then entered prison, not as a guard but as a prisoner of Christ.

Colonel Sandu Franco, a communist officer who interrogated Richard Wurmbrand in prison, came home in distress one day. Desperately holding his head, he told his wife, "Something is wrong with me! I am sick. I have never met anyone like this Wurmbrand in my life." The mind and heart of the colonel were being changed by the love of God shown by this prisoner. Colonel Franco became a Christian and later went to prison for his belief.

AFTER PRISON

———————— ⚬✾⚬ ————————

Richard Wurmbrand was released from prison in a general amnesty in 1964. On 28 November of that year, Rev W. Stuart Harris and Rev John Moseley of Mission to Europe's Millions, later to be named European Christian Mission, arrived in Bucharest. They met Richard in the German Baptist Church on Sunday evening. When the meeting was over a tall man with a slight stoop, a haggard look and a very serious expression on his face came up to them. He said, "Memorise my address and come and see me this evening. Make sure no one follows you." This was their first encounter with Richard Wurmbrand. He said how much he would like them to meet his wife and to have a longer conversation, so they agreed to his request.

Rev W Stuart Harris.

Taking what precautions they could so that they were not followed, Mr Harris and Mr Moseley made their way to the little attic home of the Wurmbrands, meeting also Sabina and their son, Michael. They had a little two-roomed flat right at the top of the building. The pastor recounted some of his prison experiences, while Michael went to look in the street below and see if anyone was watching the building. He came back with the news that the police were there.

The talk continued and then Richard Wurmbrand took off his shirt and showed them the marks on his body, both back and front. They were amazed and stunned by what they saw and heard. Then they prayed together. It was past midnight, and Mr Harris said that they must go back to their hotel. When they reached the street they found that the police had gone.

The next day they met in a park in Bucharest and had their final conversation. Precious Scriptures, a copy of Keswick Week and other items were handed over, all folded inside a communist newspaper. It was not until a year later that Pastor and Mrs Wurmbrand actually received permission to leave Romania. The communists let the family leave for a price. A ransom of $US10,000 was paid.

In the United Kingdom a couple of years later, where Pastor Wurmbrand wrote his famous book, *Tortured for Christ*, he dedicated it to Stuart Harris with these words: *To the Rev W Stuart Harris, General Director of the European Christian Mission in London, who, upon my release from prison in 1964, came to Romania as a messenger from Christians in the West. Entering our house very late at night, after having taken many precautionary measures, he brought us words of love and comfort as well as relief for families of Christian martyrs. On behalf of these faithful believers, I express our gratitude.*

In the years that followed, Mr Harris made a valuable contribution as Chairman of the international committee that guided the ministry that Richard and Sabina Wurmbrand founded.

Stuart became a friend and I am glad that during his latter years I was able to visit with him on several occasions at his home in Sheffield. One of those was his 90th birthday.

During one of these visits he told me about an experience he had during his first visit to Romania. While there he was invited to speak to the students in a small seminary the government allowed to function. It had only a small group of students and in the opinion of Mr Harris the establishment had to make concessions to the communist authorities.

He told me that after he addressed the students and spent some time with them, they lined up to shake his hand and say farewell. As he moved down the line he felt a small hard lump pressed into his palm by one of the young men. Unnoticed he slipped it into his pocket. Later, at the hotel, he discovered it was a tightly folded wad of paper. When he carefully unfolded and flattened it he discovered written on it just a couple of Bible references. Genesis 40:14, and Colossians 4:2-4.

Genesis 40:14. "But think on me when it shall be well with thee and show kindness I pray thee unto me, and make mention of me unto Pharaoh, and bring me out of this place."

Colossians 4:2-4. "Continue in prayer, and watch in the same with thanksgiving; withal praying for us, that God would open unto us a door of utterance, to speak the mystery of Christ, for which I am also in bonds: That I may make it manifest, as I ought to speak."

Note smuggled to Stuart Harris.

What the restrictions of the repressive regime did not allow the young man to say openly was adequately expressed in the Word of God. Stuart passed that historic little piece of paper on to me.

IS HELP REACHING
THE UNDERGROUND CHURCH?

The following extracts from letters received during the time of rigid communist control in the USSR and Eastern Europe (samples of many) are evidence that the families of Christian martyrs and pastors in need were being helped:

"Our beloved, once strangers, who are now so near to us in Christ Jesus. We received your parcel, for which we thank you wholeheartedly. The most important thing is to spread the news about the soon Second Coming of our King and Lord and God, Jesus Christ."

"It is difficult alone, God himself has said that it is not good for man to be alone and has made a woman as a help suitable for him. But God, wishing to try our faith and to see on what we built, He has separated us both . . . I thank the Father Who has put on your heart to send us a parcel. I and my sister-in-law were able to visit our husbands in prison. They are healthy, but surrounded by walls and eat the bread of sorrows. Thanks be to the Lord that He has given us to bear a chip of His cross."

(This seems to have become a proverbial expression among Russian Christians. We find it in several letters.)

One of our couriers wrote of the joy (as well as the natural pressure and strain) of visits to Eastern Europe. The believers behind the Iron Curtain sent greetings and grateful thanks for help received.

The courier went on: "The main objective was to take Bibles which are in very short supply. Two of the pastors who received Scriptures were like small boys at Christmas time.

"One of the highlights was meeting and conversing with representatives of the persecuted church. They had lived for many years in the frozen steppes of northern Russia and had then settled further west. From their present home they help needy believers in Russia. They take recordings from Gospel radio programmes and distribute Scriptures and funds. They are able to reach many areas of the Soviet Union and help those who need it most. The stories of suffering and persecution are very touching, but so also are the testimonies of God's wonderful working."

Another courier reports:

"Behind the Iron Curtain some too-active Christians were being persecuted. Surely it would not be long before they were in prison? So they decided to flee: a family with three children and a relative.

"I prayed very much for them. One day I got the news that they had succeeded in reaching another Communist country. The Lord spoke to my heart, 'Go and bring them over the border'.

"I went by air to Austria, rented a car and drove to the country where they were. After waiting 38 hours in a certain town, I met them on the street. What a joy! But now, how to get over the border without passports?

"We came into a terrible thunder storm and lost our way. We went up the mountain in the hope of finding the frontier-station, but in the rain the clay roads were very bad, so we became stuck in the mud. What to do? We discussed this.

"Suddenly the car was surrounded by soldiers. We were in a military area at the frontier region. The military chief was very kind to me, he didn't call the secret police, as he could have done. He understood that I had lost my way, and really I had. So in three quarters of an hour I was released. They didn't find out I had six people trying to escape. That was a new miracle. But how were we to get over the border?

"It is impossible for six people without passports, but God spoke to my heart, 'Go and bring them over the border'. We decided to pray to get God's plan. Then God spoke to my heart. I was very quiet, and full of peace.

"Now I knew where to get over and at what time: at three o'clock in the morning at a very big customs house. I knew this place and would never have tried this way by myself. There was telephone, telegraph, many customs officers and very much electric light.

"At half-past two in the morning we went on. That was the third night for the refugees without sleeping in a bed. We had to drive 30 minutes to get to the border. We prayed and the Holy Spirit immediately moved us to praise the Lord. Exactly at three o'clock we were at the border. I stopped the car, opened the window, and gave the frontier-guard my passport. He looked at it, gave it back to me and opened the bar.

"I first closed the window, and asked all to pray again because we would pass the Austrian border 500 yards away. Then I tried to drive very slowly. At the next border all the guards were very busy with some big trucks, so they had no time for us; they waved us to go on, and so God brought us to the free world.

"We went on for 15 kilometres, stopped the car, kneeled on the ground and thanked the Lord from all our hearts. Then we embraced each other and cried with joy. God had answered our prayer, 'Oh Lord, blind the eyes of the frontier guards, that they cannot see the people trying to escape!' The Lord who makes blind eyes to see had this time made seeing eyes blind."

CHINA AND SOUTHEAST ASIA

After Chairman Mao died in September 1976 many changes took place in China. The country opened for diplomatic and trade ties with the West, and tourism has become a large industry.

The new conditions facilitated the gathering of information in what was previously a closed country. One of the most exciting discoveries was the growth of the underground church, also called the house church, during the 30 dark years of Mao's rule.

Although the work was difficult, help began reaching through the Bamboo Curtain and some of the needs of our Christian brothers and sisters were met. Many people are praying and God-given wisdom is leading the way in a number of fruitful programs that have been established.

The traitorous Three-Self Committee, which controls the official church in China, the Three-Self Patriotic Movement (TSPM) – a church that co-operates with the atheistic government – continues to bring pressure to bear on the faithful house church. This involves harassment, persecution and the closure of some groups.

In 1989 we witnessed the Tiananmen Square uprising which was brutally crushed by the Chinese authorities. Since that event, pressure on the underground churches has increased and many simple Christians have been arrested. A contact of VOM was on Tiananmen Square distributing Gospel tracts to the demonstrators. He left the country on the last flight before the tanks rolled in. The Chinese Red Cross claims 2000 to 3000 people were brutally killed that night.

VOM established several secret printing facilities which produced tens of thousands of Bible study books and Gospel tracts. Our workers are in touch with thousands of Christians who worship in secluded and quiet places across the length and breadth of China.

In 1992 some of our printing presses in China were discovered by the secret police and confiscated. Some of the workers had to go into hiding for years. Since those days many new opportunities have been found to print books in China and at the time of writing, hundreds of thousands of volumes are produced and distributed across the land every year.

The hearts of the authorities remain hardened towards true freedom for Christian worship. Mao's pictures are appearing again in some places and anti-freedom, anti-capitalist-world indoctrination is being increased in schools and colleges. The government is beginning to encourage new interest in Confucianism, which Mao had stamped out as one of the "three evils". China has been working with its neighbours lately to step up the fight against terrorism, ethnic separatism, and religious extremism, a triumvirate Beijing calls "The Three Evil Forces."

In the face of these problems, our channel of help has become like a beacon of light for our suffering brethren. Just to know that we care is an encouragement.

In 1994 new restrictive regulations were legislated. This move facilitated further repressive moves against the house churches – such moves often initiated by the Three-Self Church authorities.

During the 90s a translation facility and small warehouse were established in Hong Kong. Several books, translated in Hong Kong, were printed in Australia and transported to China. By the beginning of the new century VOM had moved to two much larger warehouses, and was funding increasingly larger literature budgets to cater to the great thirst by Chinese Christians for Christian literature. A large network of contacts has been created across China within the house churches, and faithful believers are helped in many ways as couriers travel regularly to supply the great need.

Another turning point with the ministry of VOM in China was 1 July, 1997, referred to as "The Handover" when sovereignty of Hong Kong was transferred to the People's Republic of China. There were temptations to move the ministry and relocate elsewhere in Southeast Asia, but the decision to stay put proved to be the right one. Under the guiding hand of God the work remained stable through these tumultuous times, and many new opportunities were realised as the outreach continued to grow.

By the beginning of 2008 changes again occurred that led to the closure of the warehouses in Hong Kong. A number of relationships that had been established in China enabled VOM to expand its literature production and distribution within China without the need for warehouses in Hong Kong and smuggling operations across the border. The warehouses were sold to a partner in ministry who continues to use the facilities for Christian work and literature distribution.

With the Olympic Games held in Beijing in 2008, opportunities were seized and Christian literature was carried into China from VOM offices around the world. This was a supplement to work initiated on the mainland in association with leaders in the underground church.

We were informed of the arrest of many believers, especially in Beijing, in the weeks before the Olympic Games, as the Public Security Bureau (PSB) sought to limit contact of persecuted believers with foreign visitors and journalists. Pastor Bike Zhang Mingxuan, president of the Chinese House Church Alliance (known as "Bike" because he rides his bike extensively to engage in Gospel work), who was residing in Beijing to get medical attention for his wife, was approached by the PSB and offered ¥5000 ($A766.00) if he would leave the city for three

Pastor "Bike" Zhang Mingxuan.

months. When he refused, he and his wife were physically removed to Hebei County. Br Bike is a prolific distributor of Gospel tracts – as many as 35,000 a year. He is one example of many who were forcibly removed from the Olympic Games city.

After the Games, on 29 August, Bike Zhang Mingxuan and his wife were released by PSB officials. In a direct phone call from Pastor Bike to China Christian Aid President Bob Fu, Pastor Bike described the conditions and treatment since his detainment on 6 August. Bike said he and his wife were on "forced vacation" for the past three weeks, and were made to stay at four different resort locations throughout their detention.

Bob Fu, a partner with VOM, was able to speak with Bike's wife who was in excellent spirits. Mr Fu shared with the couple that since their detention a petition to have them freed had been created and signed by over 50,000 people. Bike and his wife were both excited and thankful to hear of the response from so many caring individuals. Despite the circumstances of his captivity, Pastor Bike had been actively evangelising and advocating the role of the house church to his captors. Bike and his wife were told they were prohibited from returning to Beijing until the end of the Paralympics, 16 September.

This was not the end of the matter. In October Zhang Jian, the eldest son of Pastor Bike Zhang Mingxuan, was severely beaten with iron bars at his mother's home for 25 minutes by 15 Public Security Bureau officers. Pastor Bike's wife said the plainclothes PSB officers, along with hired thugs, broke into her apartment and started throwing all of her items out on the street after she was ordered to move. Pastor Bike's younger son Zhang Chuang was badly beaten up and his mouth was swollen and bleeding. Pastor Bike was arrested as he arrived in Kunming airport, on his way to meet a VOM representative, not knowing what had transpired at his home.

In November 2008 Pastor Bike Zhang Mingxuan and other underground Christians were again targeted by authorities. On 28 November the Ministry of Civil Affairs released a statement calling for the elimination of the Chinese House Church Alliance. According to a 30 November 2008 report from China Aid Association, Pastor Zhang, the President of the Chinese House Church Alliance, was detained by four officers in Nanyang, Henan province. When authorities demanded that he sign the Ministry's statement, he refused. Seventeen Christians who were worshipping at Pastor Zhang's residence were apprehended. Although they were later released, authorities confiscated their computers, cell phones, magazines, and over 600 Bibles.

On 16 January 2009, PSB officers again forcibly evicted Pastor Bike, refusing to allow him or his family to remain in Beijing. He was put on a bus for Henan Province.

This story is recorded here as representative of the continuing persecution of Christians in China. It underscores the need to maintain the ministry begun by Pastor Richard Wurmbrand in 1967.

VIETNAM, LAOS AND BURMA

During the 90s, as the political situation in the Soviet Union and Eastern Europe changed, VOM began shifting some of its emphasis to other areas where believers faced harassment and persecution as a regular part of life. The eyes of some of its leaders fell on Vietnam and Laos and with determination and a handful of contacts, little forays into the area began. Vietnam was penetrated first, and later, as it became possible, helpful contacts were established in Laos.

As in other times and places it was soon discovered, behind the scenes, there were devoted Christians seeking to win the lost to Christ. There is an official church, which, in general terms co-operates with the atheistic government. It is largely a show church for the sake of propaganda as the country seeks to win business and tourism from the West.

As we have come to expect, we found the faithful underground church – the house churches where the Gospel is preached and the Kingdom of God extended. Alas, it can also be said, persecution, beatings and prison follow as the godless enemies of the cross seek to crush and destroy those who would dare to serve Christ.

Nevertheless, with God's help and guidance, VOM set up channels through which Bibles and Christian literature, help for pastors and their churches, equipment to enhance their ministry as well as assistance for families of martyrs flows in a steady stream. Always the need increases as through the ministry of local believers more are added to the church.

One notable achievement in 1998 was the publication, funded by VOM-USA, of the first-ever complete Bible in the Hmong language. This was to meet the needs of this large minority people group in Vietnam, Laos, China and other countries in the region.

Ministry was begun in Buddhist Burma (Myanmar) where good contacts were established. Investigative visits soon revealed a great amount of persecution of Christians. Underground house churches were discovered and with the help of dedicated Burmese Christians a literature and training ministry continues today.

Again here, VOM-USA was able to pioneer the translation and printing of a fresh revision of the Bible in Burmese. The first printing was soon distributed and a second edition was provided for clandestine distribution to Burma. Another edition was printed in 2009.

When Cyclone "Nargis" decimated parts of Burma in 2008, VOM was quickly working to help rebuild churches and give help to the shattered lives of believers. VOM-Australia gained permission from the Director General of Social Welfare in Burma and led a team who travelled by boat into the Irrawaddy Delta area. They took a few thousand backpacks loaded with clothing and food for the children and they supplied roofing iron and nails to repair churches and schools. Fishing nets, rice and farm machinery was given to Christian families. A supply of

VOM Australia delivers aid in Burma.

Bibles was distributed and tarpaulin coverings for temporary churches were supplied.

LETTERS AND COMMENTS FROM THE FIELD

"For believers in Kangaroo Country, greetings from Indonesia in the name of Jesus Christ and peaceful greetings to all Australians. My name is Hegasi and I would like to say thank you very much to Australians who have been caring through their support. I cannot repay all your kindness, but I will surrender all to the Lord Jesus who provides all we need in life. Love and greetings to all Australians and thank you very much." (VOM Australia paid medical expenses for Hegasi after she was shot in the knee during a Muslim attack.)

"When I was being persecuted, I didn't feel their insults. I was happy to suffer for the witness of Jesus Christ. I was feeling so proud of Him I didn't realize I was in pain from the beatings." – Pakistan.

"God had a purpose by allowing the Muslim young boys and girls to kill my wife. I have learned to forgive every one of them. I trust that the Lord will bless all of you who come to this remembrance service." – Nigeria.

"I have polluted and poisoned thousands of youth for 40 years. I repent. God forgive me! Pray for me, that God may use my years that remain for me to preach His Gospel of salvation." – China.

Femi Oluwasesin, whose wife was murdered by a Muslim mob in 2007: "We as a family have been overwhelmed by the number of cards that have been sent to us from all over the world. We received thousands. By this action we know that many believers are there for us, sharing our pain as a family. We are so grateful. Thank you all." – Nigeria. (In August 2008 Voice of the Christian Martyrs in Nigeria opened a computer school dedicated to the memory of Mrs Oluwasesin.)

Computer school opened in Nigeria.

"When I arrived at my grandmother's house I found they had ransacked my bedroom and stolen my carefully hidden Bible and journal. My journal was very precious to me as I had recorded my personal thoughts, scripture verses and promises of God. One entry I remember: 'Jesus I love you so much! No matter what happens to me, even if I die, I will love you forever'." – Malaysia.

"Of course we would like him to be released early, but I ask you not to pray for that. I ask you to pray for strength and dignity for us to go through this time of trial and prison, so that we may grow stronger in our faith and be worthy of Jesus' love. We pray one day we can hear Dmitry's voice and open the door and he would come there. You can make miracles. Thank you God, that we have good friends that help us live through all this." – Uzbekistan.

"It's really incredible. I think the Body of Christ is just unbelievable. And if you try to explain to someone who doesn't believe, they don't understand. But I think this is such a nice thing to see that this body of Christ is really working. And it's working together like the Lord wants us to work together and pray for one another. I really want to thank people for praying for me all over the world, especially some Americans in the United States for praying there for me and my kids and my family, for . . . really standing behind us and thinking of us as a country – thank you from my heart." – Turkey.

MINISTRY DEVELOPS IN THE MUSLIM WORLD

Richard Wurmbrand sought to talk to every man and minister to their needs. Those who embrace Islam were never outside the sphere of his love and his interest.

Even in the early days of VOM there was a quiet ministry to those believers adversely affected by attacks on their faith by militant Muslims. For many years it was a small but important part of Wurmbrand's work. There were times when he would be seen pacing the room, wringing his hands and lifting his voice in prayer when he received news of believers suffering at the hands of Islam, especially in some of the African countries.

Much of this time VOM was preoccupied with ministry in the communist world and with funding limited, not as much outreach as was needed in the Islamic world could be attempted. Where it was possible, help was given.

The first Gulf War in January and February 1991 and the buildup in the months before, presented unexpected opportunities to spread Bibles in nearby Muslim countries. During this time tens of thousands of copies of Scripture entered what were forbidden lands. Who knows what impact the Word of God will ultimately have in these places.

Since about that time there has been a notable increase in the militancy of Islam and there have been many savage attacks on Christian communities in parts of the Muslim world. VOM ministers in these places, sometimes openly providing aid to help Christians rebuild their shattered lives. In other places VOM works covertly to provide help and support with literature and funds, to strengthen the hands of courageous believers who use every opportunity to witness for Christ.

Again and again the words of Quintus Septimus Tertullian (160-240) prove to be true. "The blood of the martyrs is the seed of the church." We saw it in the communist world and again it is evident in the Muslim world. Tertullian was the first important Christian ecclesiastical writer in Latin who, while still in Rome, became a convert to the Christian faith.

Until Jesus comes again Christians will face suffering and persecution and the ministry begun by Richard Wurmbrand will continue to be a voice for those who have no voice. VOM will remain on the front lines, bringing Christian love and care to those who are persecuted for their Christian witness – those who are ready to stand up and be counted for their faith in Christ.

The work of VOM in the Muslim world takes the mission into the countries of Central Asia from Kazakhstan in the north to Pakistan and Bangladesh in the south. It embraces work throughout Indonesia, the country with the largest Muslim population in the world.

The twenty-first century witnessed the birth of the medical arm of VOM, known as VOMedical, initiated by VOM-USA. It is a sorry fact that the terror against Christians in Indonesia and other restricted nations has created much work for the medical personnel.

When the dreadful tsunami ravaged parts of Indonesia on 26 December 2004, VOM agencies instigated projects to provide help for pastors and believers and repairs to church buildings.

The African continent feels the impact of militant Islam in many places and VOM is active in Nigeria where extensive work is undertaken to help widows, orphans and remote-area pastors. There is work in Sudan, Ethiopia, Eritrea and several other countries which for reasons of security cannot be mentioned.

THE VALUE
OF RICHARD WURMBRAND'S WORK

In writing this short history, a few words should be said about the mission's founders. Sabina Wurmbrand was born into a Jewish family on 10 July, 1913 in Czernowitz, a city in the Austro-Hungarian Empire, which became a part of Romania after WWI and a part of Ukraine after WWII.

At the age of 23, in 1936, Sabina met and married Richard Wurmbrand. Shortly afterwards they were converted to the Christian faith and joined the Anglican Mission Church. At the age of 87, Sabina died on 11 August 2000.

Richard Wurmbrand was born the youngest of four boys in a Jewish family on 24 March, 1909 in Bucharest, Romania. After their ransom to the West in 1965 Richard and Sabina eventually settled in the United States, and there in 1967 they founded Jesus to the Communist World, later named Voice of the Martyrs. Richard survived his wife by six months and passed into the presence of his Lord on 17 February, 2001.

At age 87, and frail in health, Pastor Wurmbrand was forced to give up writing for the mission's monthly newsletter, something he had done without fail for 30 years. Until his death in 2001 he maintained an active interest in the work of VOM.

Michael Wurmbrand, their son, continues to work with VOM, especially encouraging survivors of the communist regime in Romania.

To indicate the value of Pastor Wurmbrand's ministry and something of the fruit which God has already given, we share some of the testimonies from letters received by our missions around the world. They speak for themselves.

Conversions

"My brothers and I were overjoyed to receive your letter and to know of the success of your work, especially that relief is getting even into the prisons. My little six-year-old has given his heart to the Lord Jesus because of hearing of Pastor Wurmbrand's love. He realized immediately that no one would suffer that much unless the Person Whom he served was real and very wonderful. So even here the Lord is using the sufferings of His dear ones to save souls. My little boy has emptied his money box for the work."

"Although I am highly regarded in my Christian circle – and thought to be one of the most dedicated – my heart is not given in an unreserved way. Your writings, reinforced by having met you personally, have caused me once more to seek God, 'that I might know Him and the power of His resurrection'. Having come to the end of your book *Tortured for Christ*, I am filled with wonder. It is a fantastic account in the sense that it is almost unbelievable: first that humans can be so beastly to each other and even more that anyone could endure such agony so cheerfully."

"I hold the work of Voice of the Martyrs very dear to myself. It was an advertisement that they placed for Mr Wurmbrand's book *Tortured for Christ* in the TV Week 30 years ago, that caught my eye. I sent away for it and, after wandering far away from the Lord, found that Christianity is for real. The witness of Mr Wurmbrand in his book compelled me to come back to the Lord and to go to church. I will be ever grateful for his amazing and compelling witness. It will be 30 years at Easter time that I came back to the things of the Lord. I can only praise the Lord for Mr and Mrs Wurmbrand's lives and the way they have brought much glory and honour to God."

"Your books have ministered to my soul as few others have, save God's Word itself. Although I have not begun to suffer the things you have, I have suffered the evil one. I shared you with my best friend who has also suffered greatly for His Name. She too was deeply ministered to through your book. God has used you as a vessel in our lives and for that we thank Him often."

"Much of the Christian church in this country is very shallow and knows little of suffering. We cannot bring comfort to one another, much less the sinful, hurting world we find ourselves in. We in this country could very well find ourselves persecuted in ways such as you experienced in Romania. God have mercy on us all."

Prayer is a great weapon

". . . we feel the time is short before our Lord's return and Satan is so busy. I feel sometimes I can do so little being crippled and unable to get about much, but prayer prevails. We shall pray not only for the suffering Christians but also for those who are causing them the suffering."

"We appreciate much what you are doing. We pray for you every morning and thank God for your mission. Through it we can reach out to the suffering. A group of us gather together monthly to pray for the persecuted."

"I have often prayed for you, your mission and for all the servants of the persecuted church. Your work is priceless, your love and mercy for others is truly Christ-like. I often daydream and wonder (because in this life you have certainly denied yourselves) about the crowns and treasures awaiting you all in the Father's Kingdom. May your work be blessed and your courage and strength be that of our Lord and King Jesus. I pray that your work may not be hindered and that God will send you all the aid necessary to continue. Many blessings to you all and God hedge and protect you wherever you go."

"I wanted to write to you, to encourage you all in the vital work that you are doing to help Christians who are being tortured and killed for their work and belief in Jesus Christ. I want to let you know that when I receive my copy of the VOM newsletter, it is opened immediately and read entirely from front to back. I pray out loud for the work of VOM and pray sincerely for every Christian who is named in the newsletter, as well as for their family and also the names of their persecutors and the prisons that our brothers or sisters in Christ are being held in."

A reality that cannot be ignored

"Thank you for the VOM update. It gives me great encouragement and keeps me in reality. We are very fortunate here in the USA, even to the point of abundance bringing us into a different captivity. Here, if we forget those whom you help and who need help, we become as one who sleeps who regards the things of God as an ordinary thing. But He is not ordinary nor His assignments nor His teachings. But they are alive and your ministry is alive and even your martyrs are more alive than those who frequent some dead churches in America. May God forgive us and bless you."

"I really appreciate your newsletter. Almost every time I read your newsletter I cry and sob, because my heart goes out with the sufferings of our brothers and sisters in Christ in many places. Your newsletter is a constant reminder to me of God's purpose."

"I would like to receive *Tortured for Christ*, as I do not have this book. Before I was afraid to read it, but I can no longer ignore the suffering in this, God's world. Also now I can see the courage of the saints and how to help."

The spiritual war

"I must express my appreciation to you and your fellow workers in Christ for the enormous encouragement that your newsletter is to me. I know that far too often and far too consistently Christians like myself get spiritually fat, lazy and comfortable. Each time I read your newsletter, however, I am reminded of the spiritual war in which we fight. It is as though a mortar shell landed just nearby and the shock waves have woken me from spiritual slumber."

"Pastor Wurmbrand's calls to love our enemies as Christ did are not only challenging to the extreme, they are also refreshingly pure in this grey and complacent society of ours. Only in Christ have I heard before of the courage, hope and love displayed by the martyrs in your newsletter. They are, as He is, a shining example and inspiration to me to continue to love, continue to pray and continue to fight for Christ and His Gospel."

"I have read some of the testimonies in the VOM newsletters and I found them to be the real thing that a true Christian is made of. I must admit many times I read them then put them down again, because sometimes I found it hard to believe that people could do those things to one another."

Challenged in great depth

"Last month for the first time I heard you speak; as a result of that my Christian life has been challenged in great depth. For three years now I have known the glorious presence of the Risen Christ, and through Him I have been able to endure the pain, both physical and mental, of living in a broken home where both my parents are drug addicts. At least, I called it pain until I heard your message . . .

"Up to the present I had no idea of the terrible conditions which my brothers and sisters in Christ were going through. I knew vaguely that some Christians did not have the same freedom of worship as I have, but I had no information . . . I find myself with a great longing to help in any way at all. I have done my best to tell others what you told us.

"On Sunday morning following your meeting, when I entered my church, I simply broke down and wept. First of all, I saw all the Bibles laid out on the Sunday school scholars' chairs, and I thought how greatly valued they would be in China. In church I was greeted by the sound of beautiful and loud organ music and singing which could be clearly heard well outside the church, yet no one rushed in to threaten us because of our faith in God.

"As we celebrated the Lord's Supper, once again I thought of all those who could not take part in this superbly beautiful service. Finally, I left the church openly carrying my Bible! From that night when you spoke

I have never been able to see a Bible, sing a chorus or hymn, or attend a Christian meeting without thinking of those who are suffering behind the Bamboo and Sugar Cane Curtains.

"Another view which has changed is the outlook I have held towards communists. For some years I have hated communism because of what it has stood for; but I went a step further. I hated the communists themselves. Now there is nothing in my heart but love for these people, and I have a great desire to see them come to know Christ as I know Him. I cannot thank you enough for the blessings I received that night you spoke."

It makes me tremble

"As we read your book, feelings of much sympathy and longing to help mingled with a sense of shame within overtook us, because we had not much idea such conditions existed, and worse still, had thought that where the truth of the Gospel was so suppressed there could not be much spiritual life.

"I have been greatly moved in reading of the suffering of our brothers and sisters of the underground church. It makes me wonder what I would do in like circumstances and it makes me tremble – I pray God will continue to preserve you and your loved ones, and also the precious believers who are so hard pressed."

Thank you for enlightening us

"We ordinary folk are completely unaware of the terrible sufferings of Christians under repressive regimes and are grateful to learn what is taking place. We believe that the Lord has raised you up to do further work for Him. Thank you for enlightening us concerning your brethren who are still suffering for Christ's sake."

"Nowadays, when our country's culture is on the brink of survival, you have, absolutely without any self-interest, supported our initiative, participating in replenishing and creating anew about 500 libraries in small villages, in military units and in prisons. This noble deed is a sign of hope and of faith in the future." – Moscow.

"I have seen the fruits of your newsletter in our midst. The dedication of Rev Wurmbrand to the souls that are suffering in the world is something that deserves our appreciation. I always read with all my heart. The stories you mention make me cry and feel real sad about our dear brothers who are suffering so much." – Angola

"The situation in Ukraine is not so tough as in Russia, but still our people live in extreme poverty. The letters our editorial office receives show how necessary our work for the people of the former Soviet Union is. Our addressees are both ordinary people and military men, also people who are now in prison. A great share of our readers are those who found Jesus Christ while reading books from our mission. We are always glad to receive more Christian literature, which we send throughout the whole country and as far as the Pacific Ocean." – Ukraine.

"I am in sincere appreciation of your VOM newsletter on such a regular basis. I am an invalid pensioner, lost my wonderful husband six years ago, but we and our entire family have a great and continued love of God the Father and His precious Son. I always read your magazines cover to cover. Thank you and may the Almighty continue to help you and yours."

"I am writing this letter to you to say thank you for sending me the information on the work that VOM does for people in the other places in the world that are persecuted for their beliefs. I would like to read more about VOM through your publications, i.e. *100 Prison Meditations*. I am in prison myself and therefore I cannot get any books from your order form. If you can help me in any way it would be much appreciated."

"I love reading your newsletters. They are so moving. When I read about Azra Bibi and Amisha in February 2008 I cried. We don't know how blessed we are here. As I live on a pension, pay increasingly more rent, I can't give any money but I can pray. I used to have a prayer group at my flat. I would love to start another one. As well as praying for people in countries like Burma and Indonesia, I'd like to pray that our young people would come to Christ. Take care now and God bless you all at VOM."

"People of the Mountains, you might be a 'Small Voice' but such a loud cry!!! Love you all! Keep up the good work. Enclosed cheque and stamps to encourage you all. Great news about Pastor Kalamevsky."

"I want to let you know that I have loved reading Richard Wurmbrand's Daily Devotional *Reaching Toward the Heights* for many years now. When I first became a Christian 25 years ago I was given the book *Tortured for Christ* by someone that I don't even remember. The effect that the book, or more accurately, the endurance of such hardship, has been part of my life ever since. God provides us with what we need and He knows what He has chosen for each of our lives, equipping us for it. Richard Wurmbrand's life has been an instrument in carrying me through some very hard situations. I read to my son's friend from the very worn daily devotional that was also handed to me eight years earlier. These words touched him so much that he now goes to a Bible study seeking after the truth."

"How tragic this June 2007 newsletter was! They are courageous folk! The poor darling lady sitting so emotionally with the food on page six. How I'd love to get her and give her one big hug! If only I could do something for her. Yet I find most people – even at church – are not interested in hearing of these sufferings. Stephen House is a wonderful project. The lovely young girls in the picture on page five. God be with them. May the Lord multiply the means that are sent you and be with you all in your great effort to help these Christians."

THE TASK AHEAD

In 1972 I met Michael Wurmbrand for the first time when I visited the office in Glendale, California. At that time he was General Director of the Mission. He has remained a friend through the years and only a few months ago, 36 years later, my wife and I spent a most enjoyable day with Michael and his wife in Los Angeles on our way home to Australia.

Michael Wurmbrand.

For years I have kept on a piece of paper in my Bible a comment that Michael once made. For me it is a constant reminder of who we are. He said, "Our chief and most immediate aim is never out of sight. It is to bring some comfort to the hundreds of thousands of people who sit in prison for their faith. We ask our friends in the free world to remember them, to 'weep with those that weep'. Jesus said that we who fail to visit the stranger, naked and ill, in prison are also neglecting Him. 'Inasmuch as ye did it not to the least of these my brethren, ye did it not to me'."

Time has passed and we now minister in the twenty-first century. Where do we go from here – what is our mission?

For me this question was answered many years ago by Sabina Wurmbrand. We were at an annual VOM conference in Germany. Lunch had just finished and Mrs Wurmbrand was sitting across the table from me, discussing the work of the mission and reminiscing a little on the path the ministry was treading. She reminded me of the vision God had given to her husband and the marvellous realisation of Richard's dream to start a mission to "take Jesus to the Communist World".

Then she paused and made a statement that has remained with me for more than two decades: *God beware us if we ever cease from caring for His little ones.* God help us if we ever stop caring for His persecuted church was her message. It was her call to us to be faithful to the vision and the calling given to our founder, Pastor Richard Wurmbrand.

This is her message and this is our calling.

INTERNATIONAL CHRISTIAN ASSOCIATION

On 3 November, 1990 the many independent missions started by Richard Wurmbrand jointly incorporated the International Christian Association (ICA) in Switzerland, and the various national offices joined the Association as members.

The purpose of the ICA is to provide an organisational tie between Christian organisations throughout the world whose founding has been inspired by Pastor Richard Wurmbrand's example and the results he achieved. The ICA requires members to adopt these main purposes:

(1) To encourage and empower Christians to fulfil the Great Commission in areas of the world where they are persecuted for their involvement in propagating the Gospel of Jesus Christ. We accomplish this by providing Bibles, literature, radio broadcasts, medical assistance and other forms of aid.

(2) To give relief to the families of Christian martyrs in these areas of the world.

(3) To undertake projects of encouragement, helping believers rebuild their lives and Christian witness in countries that have formerly suffered communist oppression.

(4) To equip local Christians to love and bring to Christ their enemies who are opposed to the Gospel in countries where believers are actively persecuted for their Christian witness.

(5) To emphasise the fellowship of all believers by informing the world of atrocities committed against Christians and by remembering their courage and faith.

History of ICA

The course of events that have brought us to this particular time in our history are quite interesting.

It should be noted that we honour Richard and Sabina Wurmbrand as our founders. However it was by the generosity of Richard's spirit that while he participated in the beginning of the USA mission, he gave people in other places the freedom to start missions independently but in fellowship with each other.

Richard Wurmbrand became known internationally mostly because of the publication and worldwide distribution of his best-selling book *Tortured for Christ*.

This led to speaking tours at the invitation of interested people in various countries. Richard Wurmbrand travelled and preached. Almost invariably as a result of his inspired preaching, hearts were moved and people wanted to do something. Richard encouraged them to start a mission in their country to help the persecuted church. He would leave the country and it was entirely for the local people to decide whether they would start something. In most cases such people gathered together a local board, went through the necessary legal procedures and founded a mission. Such new missions received a great deal of support and encouragement from the American office. Michael Wurmbrand was diligent in sending newsletters, information and photographs to the fledgling missions. In those days before computers, fax machines and email, it was all delivered regularly by air mail!

The missions were independent and the leaders largely strangers to each other.

There was no organised "umbrella" for the so-called "Wurmbrand Missions".

The Wurmbrands and Hans Braun, Director of the German mission, called a conference in 1970 to bring together the leaders of these new missions, most of whom did not know each other. The conference was held in Switzerland. From our ten-months-old mission in Australia we sent my friend and brother Reg Werry as our representative.

Conferences were then held in 1972 (Germany), 1974 (Israel), 1976 (Germany), 1978 (Switzerland), 1981 (Israel). Then annually in association with VOM offices in one country or another. Through the early years there was not an international organisation, but we met as independent missions at the invitation of Hans Braun in association with the Wurmbrand family and the U.S. mission.

A conference was planned for 1980 but at the last moment arrangements broke down. Then an emergency arrangement was made at very short notice to bring together as many mission directors as possible to meet in Oslo, Norway.

This meeting discussed the first attempt to form an umbrella organisation. It culminated in the founding of an unincorporated organisation which we called Christian Mission to the Communist World International. This was confirmed at our international conference in Israel in 1981. Following this decision the German office produced a six-page brochure outlining the constitution and main duties of Christian Mission to the Communist World International.

Meeting with Richard Wurmbrand in Norway, 1980.

We continued to work cooperatively under this agreement through the 80s. Probably it was 1989 when discussions began between Hans Braun, Hedi Fluri and myself with reference to Richard's increasing age and life expectancy. We realised that Richard and Sabina Wurmbrand somehow provided the thread that bound us together. With concerns that the missions

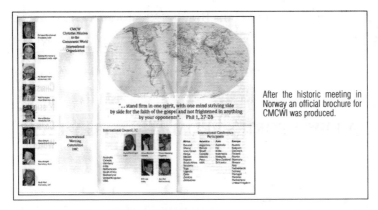

After the historic meeting in Norway an official brochure for CMCWI was produced.

could fragment after Richard's passing we discussed the possibility of founding a more legally-binding umbrella organisation which could be incorporated. Discussions continued for the best part of two years, during which time we took legal advice. In November 1990, after full and thorough discussions with the mission directors from around the world and the consent of their respective Boards, the International Christian Association was incorporated at Kreuzlingen in Switzerland.

The ICA has been through changes since that date but remains largely intact and continues to fulfil its purposes. It is important to recognise that the ICA is not a mission, but it is an association of missions. Funds remain with the missions as their responsibility to use in accordance with our vision, aims and purposes. The ICA offers a mechanism to help missions find and share projects. In March 1999 the office of incorporation was transferred from Switzerland to Oklahoma USA. Over the years some members have withdrawn and new friends have joined. There have been a number of changes to the bylaws and better and improved organisational structures have been put in place. The documents recording the founding of CMCWI and later the ICA can be found in the appendix.

We can praise God that the ICA continues to serve its purpose and is holding together in fellowship those missions whose founding was inspired by the Wurmbrand family. The ICA helps us to keep the focus of Richard and Sabina Wurmbrand to serve and support God's persecuted children.

A FEW STORIES FROM THE EARLY DAYS

I am able to present here just a few stories from the early days of our missions. They illustrate how the hand of God was with us and that in Him all things are possible.

Looking for my Brother

This is a true story told to me by a Christian friend in China: A poor farmer, a Christian, in a village far away in the mountains, heard he might be able to find a Bible in Shanghai if he contacted one of the house churches.

He packed his few belongings in a bag and made the long journey to the big city. He was poor, and when he came to Shanghai he had nowhere to stay so he just camped on the street.

After a few days people began to notice this poor country peasant. He was always there and it seemed he was just living on the street. They could tell from his rough clothing and his country accent that he was a farmer and they asked him what was he doing there, what did he want?

He told them, "I have come to find my brother." That satisfied them for a while, but as more days passed and nothing happened their curiosity grew.

"Have you found your brother yet?" they would ask. Always the answer was the same, "No, I haven't found him yet."

Days passed and the locals thought they might be able to help the poor man. They asked, "where does your brother live? – maybe we can direct you to the right street." His reply was, "I don't know my brother's address."

The people despaired and wondered how this poor peasant would find his brother in the big city of millions of people if he didn't know his address. Some of them began to laugh at him.

Others, wanting to be helpful, came to the farmer on the street and asked again, "What is your brother's name? – maybe we can put the word out to our friends and acquaintances and somebody, somewhere, might have heard of your brother."

Back came the strange reply: "I don't know my brother's name."

Now the people began to laugh and hold this poor man up to ridicule. They began to wonder if he had a problem. Maybe he was one straw short in the bale as we might say. He comes to a huge city to find his brother, but he doesn't know his address and he doesn't know his name. They began to make fun of him and soon this story was circulating in the neighbourhood. Everybody thought it was a great joke.

In a small room nearby, where an older couple were also amused, the wife paused one day and said to her husband: "You know, I was just thinking about this strange farmer down in the street. We are Christians, and as you know, we have the habit of calling our friends brother this, or sister so and so. Do you think this poor man could be sending us a message?"

The husband thought about it and a little later he went down to the street. He came to the farmer and said to him, "I hear you are looking for your brother, but you don't know his name or his address." The farmer agreed. Then the man said to him, "Do you know your father's name?" Then he paused and said, "My father's name is Abraham."

The farmer looked at the stranger, and as a tear formed in his eye he said, "My father's name is Abraham too – you must be my brother." ("Therefore be sure that it is those who are of faith who are sons of

Abraham" Galatians 3:7. "And if you belong to Christ, then you are Abraham's descendants, heirs according to promise" Galatians 3:29.)

We know that the New Testament refers to Christians as children of Abraham.

This was the right answer. Quietly this Shanghai couple helped the farmer find a smuggled Bible, and he carried this precious book home with him to his village to be the only Bible for his small house church congregation.

Not long after this event, my Chinese friend who told me this story, came along and heard about these remarkable events. He was able to get the address of the farmer and later visited him. Some time later I also visited him and working together we were able to provide a lot more Christian literature and help to what turned out to be a network of house churches in the region.

But these are the things we do, and the difficult and uncomfortable places we visit, as we go looking for our brothers. We stand beside them and support and encourage them as they get on with the business of serving the Lord in the difficult and dangerous circumstances that surround them.

It may be in China, but it could be in Indonesia or Afghanistan, Vietnam or Nigeria, or any of many restricted nations where to be a Christian is not easy. Arrest, beatings, heavy fines and other punishments await those who will be faithful to Christ. A large part of the work of VOM is to "look for our brothers". We never know where we might find them, but as God leads us along, some of these little victories are won.

All of us need to be alert to the promptings of the Spirit of God every day. Wherever we are, the Lord will put somebody in our pathway who needs our help.

Printing in the Chinese Underground

A Chinese Christian friend arranged for me to travel with him into one of the central provinces of China. He told me there was something he wanted me to see.

We got off the flight and checked into a hotel in time for lunch. After lunch he told me to go and stay in my room while he made some arrangements and he would contact me in a few hours.

I waited and the time moved on and in the late afternoon the light began to fade. I wondered what was happening and I was getting a little nervous. If something had happened to him I would be on my own and what would I do?

But I needn't have worried. About 6 o'clock there was a quiet knock on my door. I let my friend in and he told me to get my coat and my camera and be ready to leave in 15 minutes.

In the gathering darkness we climbed into a taxi that was waiting at the back entrance to the hotel. Quickly we passed through the city streets and along a dark road leading through the countryside towards the mountains. We travelled for well over an hour before the taxi stopped and we got out into the darkness. We stood alone on the side of the road until the lights from the taxi disappeared into the night as it headed back towards the city.

Then there was a movement in the bushes near the road and two or three people emerged to greet us, press our hands and murmur some words of welcome. They urged us to move quickly away from the road and with the occasional use of a flashlight led us uphill along a rough road – more like a rutted track – high into the mountains.

We arrived at a collection of small homes built in caves in the side of a valley. Here we entered one of the homes and it was good to get out of the chilly night and drink the hot tea that was offered.

First they made sure there were no unwelcome people around and then to my surprise they got down on the floor near the back wall and scraped at a few of the stones. A small section of the floor slid away to reveal the entrance to a passage leading down into the mountain.

On hands and knees I followed them as we crawled in the dirt along a long and low tunnel. After maybe 30 metres we crawled through an opening and stood up in a cavern they had dug out of the mountain. Here in this underground room was an old printing press, stacks of paper and a couple of young people very busy printing books – Christian books. In fact, at that time they were printing pages for *Tortured for Christ*.

This was a highly secret and very dangerous operation. How they got the printing machine I don't know, but I understood immediately that to get it there they had to take it apart, drag it piece by piece down the small tunnel and put it all together again. And what about the paper? In those days it was not possible to go and buy large amounts of paper, so they had to establish a network of people – each could buy just a few sheets, maybe 20 or 30, and these would then be passed along until slowly the stack grew large enough for them to begin their printing operation.

Underground printing press in Communist China.

Thankfully we don't need to do it that way any more. It is still difficult and dangerous, but it is possible to find printers who will print for us above ground and in larger quantities. It still requires both care and courage to succeed.

Well, the tour was over and we came back along the tunnel and back into the little house. Then they told me there was one more thing they wanted me to see. We made our farewells and a couple of their leaders took us along another track. We stumbled along in the darkness, but I could sense we were in some kind a field – a farmer's field of grain.

We stopped and slowly I became aware of a dark shape just ahead of me. We were out in the open and nobody really wanted to use a flashlight which might be seen by an unwelcome watcher in the neighbourhood. I realised we were beside a truck that was standing there in the middle of the field, surrounded by crops. With a shaded light they showed me a large wooden crate on the back of the truck and pressing a large old screwdriver into my hand they pushed me up beside the crate.

Using the screwdriver I was able to prize a few boards away and then, with the flashlight down inside the big wooden box, I was amazed to find a printing press – a new cylinder press covered with oily paper. I had to admire these people for the risks they were taking in their desire to improve their capacity to print Christian material for their house churches.

Peering inside crate at new press.

Well, I was taking a risk too and I quickly took a few pictures and retreated into the darkness. I learned later that they laboured all night to get the machine off the truck and onto the ground so the truck could leave before daylight. For the next few weeks there was a large haystack in that part of the field as they hid the machine. Night by night they came and got a few more pieces from it

Unpacking the cylinder press.

to drag down the tunnel where it could be put back together again and used to print more books.

It lasted a few years before the police discovered it and destroyed it and blew up the house that provided the entrance. About 40 people involved in this project had to flee and live with distant relatives. Even two or three years later their names were still on a list and they had to stay in hiding. Such is the price that some people have to pay to serve the Lord.

As for me, they put me in a taxi alone and sent me back to my hotel where I arrived very late at night. In those times, or at least in that place, guests were not given a key to their room. The attendant let you in and you could lock yourself in. When you came out, to go to breakfast or to go out of the hotel, the ever-present attendant came and locked the door.

When I returned after my late night adventure, I stepped out of the elevator and there was the attendant waiting to let me in. She unlocked the door and I stepped in. As I turned to close the door and lock it I looked back into the corridor and there on the rich red carpet I saw a line of very muddy footprints from the elevator door to my room. In the darkness I hadn't noticed how much mud was on my shoes from walking in the cornfield. It must have been obvious that I had not been walking in the city and had been away somewhere. Well, I spent the next 30 minutes scrubbing and cleaning my shoes and flushing all the dirt down the toilet. When I stepped out for breakfast in the morning I could be proud of my clean and shiny shoes!

Let us remember that every one of us will leave footprints in the pathway of life. May the marks we leave behind show we walked with the Lord and served His purposes.

Saved by the Bell in Romania

A colleague of VOM-Australia went with his wife and children to visit Hungary and Romania when the Iron Curtain was still in place. These countries were captive to the Communist world.

Our friends had relatives in Hungary which presented a good reason for going, and made it a little easier for them to get visas. They flew out of Sydney to London where they hired a camper van which would be their home for several weeks while they toured in Eastern Europe.

They visited our Swiss office as they journeyed and here they were persuaded to become part of a Bible smuggling operation. With the help of Hedi Fluri and our experienced Swiss staff, they found hiding places in their van where they could hide a quantity of Bibles. With the Bibles safely stowed, they set out on their adventure.

In Hungary they found their way to their relatives and after a nice visit for some days they drove on to cross the border into Romania. This couple had two young children, so part of their *modus operandi* was to have the children spread their books and toys and the things that amuse children all over the back of the van. They hoped this untidy mess would discourage inquisitive customs agents at the border.

It seemed to work and they safely crossed the border into Romania. Now they were people on a mission. They followed the map and some instructions to find their way to a city in Romania. Here, in due course they made contact with the people whose names they had been given – believers who were expecting the Bibles hidden in their van.

Plans were made to meet later that night on a lonely and isolated road outside the city. It was a damp night and a little bit of mist was settling when they met the other vehicle. The conditions suited what they were doing and it didn't take too long to open the secret storage places and transfer the precious goods. Then both parties went on their way.

Our VOM people drove off with something of a sigh of relief. Dangerous mission accomplished!

The next day our friends again met with some of the Romanian Christians to find they had a new proposition to put to them. The Romanians told them about the hardships being endured by their brethren in the USSR, just across the border to the north of Romania. This is what we now call Ukraine, but then it was a part of the Soviet Union. The Romanians had somehow gathered together quite a sum of money in Roubles which they wanted to give to their Soviet brothers and sisters in the underground church.

They asked our VOM friends if they would consider hiding the money in their van, drive across the border and deliver the funds. Our friends, who were not experienced in the pitfalls of such an operation, agreed to attempt this new clandestine mission.

Their van had a carpet in the back, which was held in place with a metal strip screwed down along the edge. Carefully they removed the metal strip. Then they rolled the carpet back and taking great care they spread the money in an even layer across the floor. The mat was slowly rolled back into place and the metal strip was screwed down again, and all looked normal – especially when the kids did their thing and scattered their playthings around.

They set off over poor roads about 400 km to the border.

Somehow in their inexperience and lack of understanding, or maybe it was excitement, they missed the fact that they would need visas to cross into the USSR. Perhaps they thought they could get them at the border.

Whatever they thought, they eventually arrived at the heavily guarded border crossing. There was the fence, the barbed wire, the barrier across the road and the guardhouse with many officers and a number of vehicles parked nearby.

Our driver rolled down the window as an officer approached and asked for their passports. This was the moment that our VOM friend discovered he needed visas if his family wanted to enter the Soviet Union. He asked if he could get visas there in the guardhouse, but quickly learned he would need to drive to Bucharest and make an application at the Soviet Embassy. Then he would wait at least three weeks while his application was sent to Moscow for processing. Well, he knew he didn't have that much time so he told the officer they would have to abandon the whole idea.

That was when their troubles began.

The officer said, "No, before you leave we will search your vehicle to find out what it is you want to bring into our country".

An officer put on overalls and with a flashlight in his hand rolled under the vehicle to closely examine it. At the same time another officer searched around the inside of the van, tapping the interior panels here and there, and looking in some of the closets and drawers. Our friends could only sit and wait – and trust the Lord. They knew to be discovered with such a large amount of money hidden in the van would bring serious trouble.

Then the officer stood up, looked again at the van and drew a screwdriver from his pocket. Our friends watched as he walked directly to the doorway and placed his screwdriver on the first screw holding the metal strip on the carpet. It seemed their project was going to be discovered and they silently prayed that God would help them to handle the questions that would begin in just a few minutes. "Each day has enough trouble of its own" as we read in Matthew.

While all this was happening, the phone rang in the guardhouse. An officer picked up the phone and said a few words, then he opened the office window and called loudly to the man with the screwdriver. He was wanted on the phone.

Our driver watched him as he walked to the building to take the call, and he thought to himself, "well, I have a few more minutes to pray!"

Then he watched as the examining officer talked, and talked, and talked, and waved his fist, and the screwdriver, and shouted and so it went on, and on, and on . . .

And all the time our friends sat in the van and waited.

Eventually the conversation ended. They could see the officer through the window. He just stood there with his back to them. Then he turned around and saw them. With an angry gesture he waved at them as though to say, "What are you doing? Get out of here!"

They didn't need to be told a second time and with a silent prayer of thanks to God they went on their way. You could say they were saved by the bell – the telephone bell!

I remember the words we find in the book of Isaiah – "It will also come to pass that before they call, I will answer; and while they are still speaking, I will hear" Isaiah 65:24.

Wet weather in Vietnam?

On a Sunday morning about 6.30 we crept out of the hotel in Saigon, walked down the street and turned into a narrow lane to another street and then quickly slipped into a van that was waiting for us. The driver took us north towards the highlands. We were on our way to visit a church, but the journey along narrow and rough roads took longer than we expected and we arrived late – after their service. They told us there had been about 70 in attendance at the meeting. This church they built without permission and they continue their activities without permission, but generally-speaking the police tolerate them and most of the time leave them alone. Just from time to time they visit and harass them. However, if we had been found there it might not have gone well with the authorities and it seemed better for us to move on. They invited us to come for lunch on the next day, so we moved on after a short visit.

A few miles further along we turned off the main road and drove through some narrow, rough, dirt lanes to visit a house church that would be meeting in the afternoon. These were people from the Mnong tribe. Contact with foreigners is forbidden and they were not allowed to have any printed material in their own language.

As we got near to the place thunder and lightning filled the sky and rain began to pour down on us. We had to rush from the van to the door of the house through torrents of rain. The lightning and thunder continued and it fairly teemed as we were welcomed into the crowded house. We began to apologize to the people, but they assured us they felt very happy about this situation as they were sure it would prevent the police from disturbing them. With such heavy rain, they said, the police would much rather stay in their dry office than come out in the storm to look for them.

They explained that the police regarded their meetings as totally illegal and it would be especially bad for them if foreigners were found to be present. It would surely mean some of them would be arrested and would go to jail. Nevertheless they were delighted to welcome us and have us participate in their house church meeting. Indeed this really was a house church. The authorities would not allow them to build any kind of church building, so they met in somebody's house.

As we entered the house and shook the rain off, they indicated we should climb the stairs to the attic. Upstairs was a single room of about 30 square metres and already about 50 people had jammed into the space. It was hot and humid. The temperature was in the 40s (over 100°F) and the rain was thundering down, here and there dripping through the thatch of the roof and it was like being in a sauna. We were glad it was not an iron roof because it would have been impossible to hear anything above the rattle of the rain. The people were overjoyed to meet us and to welcome us. It was the first time ever for them to have visitors from the West. Several of the visitors brought greetings and messages – which had to be translated from English to Vietnamese and then from Vietnamese to Mnong. At the end of the meeting their ladies' choir sang ("I am His and He is mine forever") in Mnong.

During the meeting we noticed nobody seemed to be holding a Bible

and as we talked to the leaders afterwards we asked them about this. They told us it was true – nobody had a Bible, because the Bible had never been translated and printed in their language. We talked to an older man who told us he had been in prison because the police caught him evangelising from one village to another. He told us some of them had been translating parts of the Bible and now they had nearly one complete handwritten copy of the New Testament. It needed only one more revision and it would be ready for printing – but they had no money to publish it. We rejoiced that VOM could take this as a project and a few months later the first 1000 copies were printed and after more revisions and checks further editions were published. Can you understand what it means to receive the first-ever printed copies of God's Word? In the West we practically swim in Bibles. Here were people who had never had God's Word for themselves

Handwritten Mnong New Testament

and what a privilege to work with them to provide them with this precious book for the first time.

Well, it was time to go and we climbed back into our van, but the ground was so slippery with the rain that the van slipped and slithered as the driver tried to negotiate the slope up to the gate. We went sideways with the wheels spinning and it seemed to be impossible to steer between the narrow gateposts. The Lord was with us and after three or four attempts the van straightened up and glided steadily in a straight line through the gateway and into the muddy laneway. By the grace of God we made it along several slippery lanes and around a couple of bends and then onto the main road – and we were away down the highway, sometimes through 150 mm of water across the road.

Less than 20 km along the road we ran into perfectly dry conditions. There hadn't been a drop of rain and it seemed to confirm the villagers' belief that the Lord had sent the rain, just where it was needed, to keep the police away and to allow us to meet safely.

That evening we reflected on the eventful day, and the way we crept carefully into the church meeting and then slipped and slithered away. We thanked God for believers who find that Jesus Christ is so real to them that they will risk everything for Him.

Buying Stamps in Communist China

China had been tucked away behind the "bamboo curtain" for decades and nobody knew with certainty what the future would bring. Many wondered what kind of religious activity was happening. They wondered if the small flickering light of Christianity that had existed in China in the 1940s had been snuffed out when Mao came to power in 1949.

It was into this atmosphere that our pioneering group stepped in 1980.

Through a Chinese contact, arrangements had been made to use a tour group in an attempt to carry a quantity of Bibles across the border, hidden in their luggage. The tourists would check into a tourist hotel and a secret Christian would contact them to take delivery of the precious cargo.

God's hand was on the group and they succeeded in getting safely through all the security checks and eventually arrived at an inland city where they checked into their pre-booked hotel. It seemed all was well.

However, a day passed but nobody contacted them. Then another day went by and still nobody came looking for them. They were nervous about leaving the Bibles hidden in their rooms, but they could not stay there all the time. If they wanted to look like tourists they had to be out and about. Usually somebody stayed behind, but still nobody came to find them. It seemed there had been a problem with the arrangements, or they were being watched and their contact was afraid to come.

What could they do? They couldn't ask somebody where to find the local house church. They could pray and they prayed a lot.

The leader remembered he had promised to bring his daughter some postage stamps from China. With nothing else to do he decided he could at least find the Post Office. Nearby there was a small, fairly simple tourist shop, where he knew the owner spoke a little English. He entered the shop to ask for directions to the Post Office.

The owner wanted to be helpful so he insisted on closing his shop and taking the tourists to the Post Office, saying it was difficult to find and it would be better if he showed them the way. So they all went to the Post Office.

Our group leader bought his stamps and thanked the shopkeeper and said they would now return to their hotel. The shopkeeper wanted to go with them – maybe he wanted to continue practicing his English! So they all returned to the hotel and they invited their guide to come with them into one of their rooms.

He stayed with them chatting for a short time, then said he must return to his shop. As he turned to go, one of the group experienced a moment of guilt. They had walked and talked with this Chinese man for nearly an hour and none of them had said anything to him about his soul or about eternity. He plucked up courage and as the man turned away to leave he touched him on the shoulder and asked him, "Have you ever heard of Jesus".

The Chinese shopkeeper stopped as though he had turned to stone, then with his eyes wide open he looked at the speaker and asked, "Are you a Christian?"

The speaker replied, "Yes, I'm a Christian." With tears running down his face the Chinese man said "I didn't know there were Christians outside of China!"

It was a wonderful experience as East met West in a time of rejoicing. Then our tour leader told the Chinese man about their problem and asked if he knew where they might find a house church, an underground church, somewhere in the city.

The man smiled as he replied, "Yes there is a house church in the city. It meets in the room behind my shop, and I am the leader."

Late that night some of the group crept into the room behind the darkened shop where they had a short time of Christian fellowship. They delivered their precious cargo to tearful men and women who for years had prayed asking the Lord to help them find some Bibles.

"Be strong and courageous, do not be afraid or tremble at them, for the Lord your God is the one who goes with you. He will not fail you or forsake you" Deuteronomy 31:6.

Indeed the Lord had been with them and had not forsaken them on their journey.

Leningrad: "Can you give me a Bible?"

In 1974 in Israel, at one of our first conferences, I sat and listened to a man I had met only briefly once before. He later became a good friend and brother in the Lord.

He said, "I have just come back from Leningrad . . ."

His story went something like this: He led a tourist group to Leningrad (now St. Petersburg) in what was then the Soviet Union. Between them, spread through their suitcases they had about 700 Russian Bibles. In the goodness of God they passed safely through Customs and went to their hotel.

It had been arranged that somebody from the underground church would meet them and take delivery of the precious goods. But something went wrong and the person never came. They waited a few days, always making sure somebody was at the hotel. But it was all in vain. Nobody came!

The leader of the group decided they should all go to visit a cultural exhibition that was advertised in the city of Leningrad and after breakfast they made their way to the location. They found a German-speaking guide to lead them.

Meanwhile, some time before this, an elderly couple who worked for the trans-Siberian railroad, and who lived in some inhospitable place in the icy wastes of Siberia, were approached by the leader of the underground church where they worshipped.

He reminded them that as free workers they were entitled to annual holidays when they could take a free journey anywhere on the Soviet rail system. As it was time for their vacation, he asked them if they would use this as an opportunity to serve the Lord. He went on to explain that they had no Bibles, or maybe one or two, and he had heard that in far off Latvia, in the city of Riga, a few Bibles were available at the Baptist Church. His question was would they use their holiday trip to ride the train to Latvia and bring back a few Bibles for their congregation?

They agreed.

So they made the long west-bound trip. First several days to Leningrad. A change of trains and a long overnight journey to Riga.

They went to the Baptist Church but alas, there were no Bibles. It was only a rumour. Disappointed, they began the long return journey to the East.

First they had to return to Leningrad. Here they discovered they had to wait until very late at night for a train going to the place where they lived. They sat at the Leningrad train station and waited . . . and waited. Eventually the man said to his wife, "Why should we sit here all day? Let us go into the city and see something." Then they noticed a poster advertising a cultural exhibition and decided that is where they would start.

So they arrived at the exhibition hall and went in. Soon they noticed a foreign tour group and they could hear the guide speaking in German, a language they understood. They attached themselves to the group and moved with them from one display to another.

My friend, the tour leader told us, "As we moved around the cultural exhibition, I noticed an elderly couple were standing near me, listening to the explanation given by our guide. When our group moved, they moved too.

"In a while I felt a touch on my elbow. I looked around and here was this elderly man. He asked me, 'You are from Germany?'

"I answered 'yes' and walked on.

"We listened to the guide, and soon I felt another touch on my elbow. It was the same man and he asked another question: 'Are you a Christian?'"

Our tour leader answered, "yes" and again walked on.

It wasn't long and again he felt the touch on his elbow, and the stranger whispered, "Can you give me a Bible?"

With that the whole story came out. They took the couple to their hotel that evening and many tears flowed as this elderly couple from Siberia received not a Bible, but 700 Bibles to take with them on the train later that night.

During the years that followed many such events took place – in the Soviet Union, in Eastern Europe, and later in China – as we witnessed the hand of God at work in our midst. The work was hard and it was a triumph to take even one suitcase of Bibles across a hostile border to bless the thirsty souls in a foreign land.

"And the Lord is the one who goes ahead of you; He will be with you. He will not fail you or forsake you. Do not fear, or be dismayed" Deuteronomy 31:8.

"Go to Indonesia"

In the 1970s I received a message from Richard Wurmbrand advising me that I should visit a certain lady in Indonesia with a view to starting a mission in that country.

He gave me a name and address and little other information. In due time I wrote and arranged to meet this lady in Indonesia. I wondered how this contact had come about and what story might lie behind this request.

Mrs Hadinato met me at Jakarta airport and took me to the lovely home where she lived with her husband and family. I felt there was a story behind this encounter and began to ask questions. I sought to find out what I might possibly be able to do to help with the formation of a mission to help the persecuted church, if that was her desire.

She told me a remarkable story.

Some time previously she had been encouraged to read a book given to her by a friend. The name of the book was *In God's Underground* by Richard Wurmbrand.

As she read the book she was intrigued and very moved but began to wonder if it was a true story, or something the writer had invented only to make money. She questioned how such things as were described in the book could be true. Mrs Hadinato and her husband were planning a business trip to America, so she called ahead to Richard Wurmbrand's office asking if she could meet him. Whoever answered the phone said it would not be a problem and just to call when she arrived in Los Angeles.

A few weeks later Mrs Hadinato called from her hotel in Los Angeles only to be told there was no possibility of meeting Pastor Wurmbrand. Her first reaction was to think to herself she had been right all the time. The book that had challenged her heart was a hoax – just a story to make money. Although she was disappointed, she tried again some days later, but the answer was the same. She was convinced she was wasting her time.

The couple moved on to San Francisco and somehow Mrs Hadinato felt constrained to make one more attempt, so again she called the mission office in Los Angeles. This time, in the plan of God, Michael Wurmbrand answered the phone. He listened to her story and then assured her that his father would be willing to meet her, but in fact he was travelling for meetings throughout America. Mrs Hadinato asked if she could have his itinerary in case, during their travels, there would be an opportunity to go to one of his meetings.

Michael replied in the affirmative and the first thing he said was "At the moment my father is in San Francisco . . ." That was as far as he got when he was interrupted with the exclamation, "Why! that is where I am calling from. Tell me where he is preaching and I will go and hear him." Michael said, "I can do better. I will give you the name of his hotel and his room number and you can call him."

To illustrate the wonder of God's way of doing things, it was the hotel Mrs Hadinato was calling from and the room was just down the corridor!

That evening Mr and Mrs Hadinato had dinner with Richard and Sabina Wurmbrand. They were overwhelmed with the meeting and convinced of the authenticity of the man and his message. Mrs Hadinato wanted to start a mission in Indonesia to encourage help for the persecuted church. So Richard wrote to me and asked me to visit her.

"This was the Lord's doing, and it is marvellous in our eyes?" Mark 12:11.

During the next few years Mrs Hadinato arranged the translation into Indonesian and the publication of all of the Wurmbrand books to that time. She also produced a newsletter. After some years her husband became ill and passed away and she was not able to continue the ministry. She helped us find the young man to replace her and he has faithfully and wonderfully continued and expanded the ministry in Indonesia to this day.

Wet paper in the Philippines

During the first ten years of the mission in Australia I became interested in the Philippines. The activities of the Communist Party, and especially their military wing, the New People's Army, was getting coverage in our newspapers.

We had special literature written by Pastor Wurmbrand that I knew would be helpful in this situation. But the question was how to get a foothold in the country. I had a friend, an Australian evangelist who had ministry in the Philippines and went there periodically for evangelistic meetings throughout the islands. Eric agreed to take me with him.

A week or two before we left violence erupted in the Philippines and I asked Eric, "Do you think under the circumstances we should still go?" Eric looked at me and said quietly, "Anywhere with Jesus I can safely go." End of conversation.

We arrived in Manila and settled into our hotel. Over the meal, Eric asked me for my passport and tickets so he could reconfirm the next day's flight. That was when I discovered I had left my travel documents in the taxi. What a dilemma! Eric said, "Let's pray about this and finish eating." He proceeded with a simple prayer asking for the Lord's help. Before we finished our meal, the taxi driver stood at out table to offer me my travel wallet. I discovered later he had already taken his reward, in addition to the one I gave him. But it didn't matter. I was thankful to the Lord for His rescue.

I travelled with Eric to various meetings hoping to meet somebody who might give VOM a beachhead in this needy country. Nothing very promising seemed to happen. Then we travelled to the island of Mindanao where Eric and his team had meetings arranged.

At one of these meetings I met a young pastor named Eddie who seemed to be sure he should somehow work for VOM and do something to share our message from the persecuted church to the Filipinos. In fact he did become our representative and was responsible during the next few years for distributing hundreds of thousands of Richard Wurmbrand's special publications. Eddie arranged translation into

Tagalog and Cebuano, and the books were printed in Australia and shipped to the Philippines.

I visited with Eddie on numerous occasions and he told me his story.

Years before his father had a book, but it was in English and he couldn't read it and he put it aside. Then it was discarded and ended somewhere in a pool of water. This was when Eddie found it and he took it out of the water, curious to see what it was. Carefully he separated the pages and laid them out on the rocks to dry. Then he read it. It was *Tortured for Christ* by Richard Wurmbrand. As he came to the back cover he found a sticker with the name of VOM Australia on it.

Eddie was moved by the book and wanted to do something, but didn't know where to start. Then I came to an evangelistic meeting and was introduced as being from VOM in Australia. For Eddie this was the answer to his prayers and this is why he was so sure he had to work with us.

Eddie did a marvellous job, but suddenly and sadly somebody entered his house one night and shot his wife dead, leaving him with five children. The word around was that his life also was in danger. In fact it was suggested the bullet had been meant for him. We can only speculate that the half-million or so books he had distributed had upset somebody. Eddie took his children and moved overseas to be near his sister. VOM gave him some help for a time until he became established.

We cannot always understand the things that God does. We walk by faith and not by sight and are grateful that we had an opportunity to share our special message with people in the Philippines.

"My times are in Thy hand; Deliver me from the hand of my enemies, and from those who persecute me" Psalm 31:15.

TIMELINE

In Hebrews 13:3, God's Word instructs us to *"Remember them that are in bonds, as bound with them; and them which suffer adversity, as being yourselves also in the body."* God knew that His children would suffer for their faith. He knew that thousands of His children would be imprisoned, beaten, tortured, and martyred for their Christian testimony.

Richard Wurmbrand often reminded us that when God's children suffer, He suffers too. He feels the pain. As we share with our persecuted brothers and sisters, there is a way in which we also share in the sufferings of our Saviour. *"That I may know him, and the power of his resurrection, and the fellowship of his sufferings, being made conformable unto his death;"* Philippians 3:10.

God also knew that it would be necessary for those living in a free society to share in the suffering of others, by remembering those in bonds and by reaffirming that our citizenship is in heaven and not in this world. God knew that by sharing in the suffering of others, we would be better prepared to endure such trials, and that we would strengthen the whole Body and fulfil His Word. *". . . whether one member suffers, all the members suffer with it; or if one member be honoured, all the members rejoice with it"* 1 Corinthians 12:26.

On the following pages is a timeline of some of the known events that led to the establishment of Voice of the Martyrs and its continuing ministry. It is not to rejoice in our own efforts, but rather to reveal

God's intimate work in putting together all the necessary pieces to accomplish His desire.

Prior to 1937

In one of the many mountain villages of Romania lived a godly old carpenter named Christian Wölfkes. He had a fervent love for the Jews and desired above all else that before he died he would be able to win a Jew for Christ. But there were no Jews in his village, he was ill and had no strength to travel in search of any Jew to whom he could testify. In a wonderful way, God would fulfil his desire.

1937

Seeking medical recuperation, a young Jewish man and his wife arrive in the village. There, for the first time in their lives, the embittered couple encounter a man who simply lavishes love and kindness upon them. For hours the old carpenter prays for these Jewish strangers and seeks, by all means possible, to lead them to the Saviour. In a final effort to convert the young Jewish couple, the elderly carpenter gives them his New Testament.

1938

Love triumphs: the Jewish strangers, Richard and Sabina Wurmbrand, dedicate their lives to Jesus Christ and His service.

1941

Romania supports Germany in the war against the USSR and is host to German forces. Richard Wurmbrand, now a pastor, sees a new opportunity among the occupying soldiers and engages in evangelistic activities.

Before long the Wurmbrands learn what it means to suffer for Christ. During the Nazi terror they are repeatedly beaten and arrested. Mrs Wurmbrand's family perishes in the mass extermination of Jews within the Nazi concentration camps.

1944

Romanian communists "liberate" Romania and a million "invited" Russian troops pour into the country. Pastor Wurmbrand engages in a twofold ministry – to his own oppressed countrymen and to the Russians. He boards trains and uses the long journeys to preach the Gospel; in disguise he goes into Russian army camps and expounds the Word of God. Richard arranges the secret printing of one million Russian Gospels disguised as communist propaganda.

1945

Pastor Richard and Sabina Wurmbrand attend the "Congress of Cults" arranged by the new Romanian Communist government. As many religious leaders come forward to swear loyalty to the new regime, Sabina Wurmbrand tells her husband to "wipe the shame from the face of Jesus." Richard, knowing the outcome of such an act, tells his wife that if he challenges the congress she will no longer have a husband. Her only reply is, "I don't need a coward for a husband." When the pastor steps forward the delegates believe he will also praise the new leadership, but to their surprise, Richard tells the 4000 delegates that their duty as Christians is to glorify God and Christ alone.

1946

Knowing the dangers of evangelical activities, Pastor Wurmbrand leads an underground church to encourage the faithful believers and pursue his missionary endeavors among the Russian soldiers. He believes God has sent the Russians to Romania that they might be saved.

1947

Richard organises groups of Christians to smuggle Russian Gospels into the Soviet Union. Although he is a marked man, he vigorously continues his underground church work. On 30 December, the People's Republic of Romania is proclaimed.

1948

On Sunday morning, 29 February, Pastor Wurmbrand leaves for church. He never arrives. A small group of secret police, accompanied by the governor, kidnap Richard and take him to their headquarters. He is locked in a solitary cell and assigned "Prisoner Number One".

Official prison picture of Richard Wurmbrand.

1949

Chairman Mao stands above Tiananmen Square in Beijing on 1 October and declares "The Chinese people have stood up" as he inaugurates the People's Republic of China.

1950

Aware of Sabina's work in the underground church, the communists arrest her and assign her to forced labour on the Danube Canal. Her 11-year-old son Mihai, is left orphaned. The Wurmbrand flat is seized by the police and Michael is turned into the street. Alice Panaiodor takes him into her small home.

1953

Sabina Wurmbrand is released and continues her work in the underground church. She is told that her husband has died in prison. Refusing to believe the report, Sabina retains her hope of one day seeing Richard again.

1956

Despite the treatment he receives from his captors, Richard treats them only with kindness, just as the old carpenter treated him years before. In a general amnesty, Richard Wurmbrand is released after serving eight-and-a-half years in prison. He had endured horrific tortures at the hands of the brutal secret police who warned him to never preach again. After his release, Richard immediately resumes his work in the underground church.

1959

Richard is turned over to the authorities by one of his own associates in the underground church. He is re-arrested and sentenced to 25 years. Alice Panaiodor is arrested and serves five years in prison. In her book *Walk Through Flames* she later describes in graphic detail the awful degradation of her prison experience.

1964

Pastor Wurmbrand is released from prison in another general amnesty and resumes his work. Alice Panaiodor is released and returns to Bucharest. Rev W Stuart Harris and Rev John Moseley of Mission to Europe's Millions, later named European Christian Mission, arrive in Bucharest. Taking care that they are not followed, Mr Harris and Mr Moseley make their way to the little attic home of the Wurmbrands. The pastor recounts some of his prison experiences, while his son, Mihai (Michael), looks in the street below to see if anyone is watching. The police are there. The next day they meet in a park in Bucharest and have their final conversation. Precious Scriptures and other items, folded in a communist newspaper, are handed over. This is the first contact the Wurmbrands have had with outside missionaries since their arrests.

1965

The Wurmbrand family is ransomed from Romania for $US10,000 and Richard is again warned by the secret police to remain silent about his experiences. The Wurmbrands travel to Scandinavia and then to England where they live under the care of the Harris family for several months. While in England, Richard writes *Tortured for Christ*. They continue on to the United States. Richard is arrested at an antiwar demonstration on the Berkeley campus of UCLA, after forcing the microphone from the moderator's hands in front of an angry mob. Police arrest him to "rescue" him from the angry crowd. They quickly release him. The incident goes on nationwide news. In May, the pastor testifies in Washington DC before the Senate's Internal Security Subcommittee, stripping to the waist and revealing eighteen deep torture wounds on his body. His story spreads rapidly across the country, and the world, and hundreds of speaking requests arrive at his home.

1966

Richard and Sabina begin an international speaking tour, revealing the atrocities committed against their brothers and sisters in communist countries. Pastor Wurmbrand learns that the Romanian secret police are plotting his assassination. Even with the continued threat of danger, the pastor cannot be silenced. He continues his speaking tour and becomes known as "The Voice of the Underground Church" and "The Iron Curtain St Paul."

1967

Desiring to serve their persecuted family in a greater way, the Wurmbrands officially begin a ministry committed to this service. In April, Jesus to the Communist World, later to be named Voice of the Martyrs, is formed. *Tortured for Christ*, a book highlighting Pastor Wurmbrand's testimony, is released. In October, the first issue of The Voice of the Martyrs monthly newsletter is published in the USA. The Communist Party in Albania closes all churches and declares itself the first "atheist state".

1968

In the Netherlands a group of businessmen buy 20,000 copies of *Tortured for Christ* to give out freely on campuses to counteract communist propaganda. Secret underground printing press discovered in the village of Torun in Ukraine. The mission begins secret work in China.

First issue of Voice of the Martyrs Australian monthly newsletter.

1969

The desire to assist the persecuted church spreads rapidly as Christian men and women approach Richard, offering to leave secular careers and businesses to further the work of VOM. In August Richard Wurmbrand makes

Preaching at St. John's Parramatta, NSW.

his first visit to Australia. Offices are opened in Germany, Switzerland, The Netherlands, England, Australia, New Zealand, and South Africa. Within the next few years VOM missions also begin in Canada, Belgium, India, Sweden, Finland, Italy, Portugal, and other countries. VOM launches balloons carrying Gospels into China and North Korea. The first Australian newsletter is produced.

1970

Wurmbrand continues to speak about the jailing of Christians in inhumane conditions in the Soviet Bloc. Communist guerrillas terrorise Christians in Argentina, Colombia, Uruguay and Guatemala. The church continues to win young people to

The mark of the Red Dragon: This Riazan prison, Soviet Union, built in the 18th Century is still in use. The Baptist Oleg Popov is among the Christians kept there.

Christ, threatening the power base for communist authority. VOM equips Christians with Bibles and literature to share Christ with their enemies. The first conference of international missions begun by the Wurmbrand family meets in Switzerland. Alice Panaiodor, who had been released from prison, is helped by the Wurmbrands to leave Romania. Richard and Sabina visit Australia.

1971

Christians across Russia and Eastern Europe are jailed and put into asylums for the insane. Church buildings are closed, but Russia has the fastest-growing church in Europe. Wurmbrand reports on letters received from Sudan about communist terror and churches being burned down.

Romanian Baptist Dumitru Muresan declared insane.

1972

Russian hymn books printed in Australia.

Russian song books are written by hand because of the lack of printed materials. VOM smuggles song books and literature into Russia. Romanian communists publicly declare, "The duty of the church is to fight against Wurmbrand." Most North Koreans do not have radios, so a powerful amplifier is set up on the border between South Korea and North Korea to broadcast the Gospel. In Germany the second international conference of the missions is held, with the commitment to meet every two years.

1973

Spanish tracts are dropped off boats and floated into Cuba with help from Tom White. The Chinese Communist government orders all unregistered churches to close. Secret baptisms in the Soviet Union lead to arrests.

Underground Church baptism in Russia.

1974

Somalia, Ethiopia, South Yemen, Iraq, Angola and Mozambique pass into communist hands even as VOM sends 30,000 New Testaments into Angola and Mozambique. The mission's international conference is held in Jerusalem.

1975

The Soviets make a movie against Jesus to the Communist World (VOM). Debate about Wurmbrand rages – the Communist newspaper *Sovietskaia Bielorussia* attacks him for smuggling Bibles into the Soviet Union. Christians burnt alive in Chad. VOM sends 42,000 Gospels into Red China.

Secret printing house in Soviet Union.

1976

As many Cambodian Christians flee from attack, VOM supplies them with rice. The German mission produces three volumes of illustrated Bible stories for Soviet children. Secret printing shops are created in three more countries. VOM smuggles a film out of Russia, vividly showing a Soviet concentration camp. The film is shown on national TV networks.

1977

Notice of fine for attending prayer meeting.

Russian children are put into psychiatric asylums for refusing to deny Christ. Communists declare there are two devils – Sakharov and Wurmbrand. Because of his book *Was Karl Marx a Satanist?* Wurmbrand is called a "devilish pastor". Planes drop Gospels over African guerrillas. VOM receives letters of appreciation confirming its work in Nigeria, Belize, Ghana, Chile, Red China and other countries.

1978

Ethiopia witnesses the mass murder of Christians by communists. Families of martyrs are helped by VOM. Richard Wurmbrand visits Australia for the fifth time. Old and young Baptist believers in Omsk in the Soviet Union savagely beaten while celebrating Easter. Believers fined for attending prayer meetings. Our Swiss mission receives a bomb threat from a terrorist group.

1979

In Ethiopia Christian prisoners are tortured with boiling oil and have their eyes sewn shut. Rather than abandoning their faith, they are busy with Bible distribution as never before. Tom White and Mel Bailey are captured in Cuba after dropping Gospel tracts from their plane. Both are sentenced to 24 years in prison. Secret printing shops are started in three more countries. Literature spreads to Emirates in the Arabian Gulf.

Tom White

1980

VOM begins work in Afghanistan and Nicaragua. Tom White and Mel Bailey released from Cuban prison and returned to USA after the intervention of Mother Teresa and letters from VOM supporters around the world. 12,000 books and 800 Bibles secretly introduced to Albania and contact established with underground church. Sabotage attempt on VOM radio installation in Italy. By now the mission publishes our literature in Estonian, Russian, Romanian, Hungarian, Polish, Arabic, Chinese and Vietnamese. Meeting in Norway, the directors of many VOM offices organised the first unincorporated association of "Wurmbrand" missions as Christian Mission to the Communist World International. The national offices commit to work together and to meet annually for fellowship and discussion. Hans Braun takes on the role of secretary of the new organisation.

A Christian sister being arrested in Moscow.

1981

Soviet Christians are arrested and tortured. Christians in Iran are slaughtered by Islamic fanatics. VOM responds by being a voice for the persecuted church. In Ethiopia the Christian emperor Haile Selassie murdered and many Christians imprisoned or killed. VOM puts in place a project enabling supporters to send letters to Russian Christians in their own language. Communists in Colombia murder Chester Bitterman of Wycliffe Bible Translators. The Wurmbrands make their last visit to Australia.

Soviet police interrupt underground church meeting and arrest participants.

1982

VOM prints Christian literature in more than 20 Indian languages. Literature is spread in Nepal, Bhutan, Pakistan and Bangladesh. In Poland, Christians pack their churches even though many clergy are beaten and arrested. VOM sends Christian anti-communist literature. Believers pray in fields in Czechoslovakia. VOM helps their children with food, toys and books. Six underground printing presses are at work in China printing hymnals, Gospels and Christian books. Russian Baptist pastor Nikolai Hrapov dies in jail after 28 years of detention, and arrests of Soviet Christians continues.

Some of VOM's literature.

1983

VOM smuggles small books about Christ to Tibet. Thousands of evangelicals are murdered in Nicaragua by Sandinistas (Marxist guerrillas). VOM helps Nicaraguan Christians carry in literature to share Christ with their enemies. VOM-Australia distributes Richard Wurmbrand's writings in the Philippines. Christians imprisoned in Czechoslovakia. VOM-Australia prints books for Sri Lanka, Russia, Tibet and Poland.

1984

Three hundred pastors in Ethiopia have passed through prisons. The few churches left open are full, especially with youth. The

"Sendero Luminoso" or Shining Path communist guerrillas in Peru, Colombia, Ecuador, El Salvador and Nicaragua terrorize poor villages and hunt down Christians who threaten their power. Romanian newspaper *Scinteia Tineratului* writes against

Wurmbrand's book *Answer to Moscow's Bible*. VOM-Australia open new office in Penrith.

1985

In the USSR, prisoners are drugged to elicit false confessions, children are forced to testify against their parents and a majestic cathedral is converted into a Museum of Atheism. VOM encourages readers to write to prisoners. Enver Hoxha, dictator of Stalinist Albania dies. Ethiopia reports 1500 churches closed.

Home-made printing machine.

VOM helps 1600 house churches in China. Michal Horev, underground Baptist leader in Soviet Union, receives fourth prison sentence. Secret printing continues in the USSR.

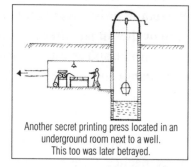

Another secret printing press located in an underground room next to a well. This too was later betrayed.

1986

Christians in East Germany suffer behind the Iron Curtain. A church is dynamited to make room for more construction of the Berlin Wall. VOM distributes Arabic and Turkish literature in Sudan, Egypt and Turkey. Ukrainian Baptist Balzky sentenced third time for giving religious instruction to youth. VOM distributes hymn books in China. Reported that 12,000 Christians are in prison in Mozambique. Chinese Christian who spent 28 years in prison meets with Richard Wurmbrand.

Church dynamited.

1987

Reforms begin in the Soviet empire and President Mikhail Gorbachev introduces *glasnost* and *perestroika*, bringing increased freedoms in the USSR. Starving Mozambican Christians ask for canoes to travel the rivers to share the Gospel with their communist enemies. VOM provides the canoes as well as food and clothing. VOM literature is translated into Urdu for Pakistan. VOM provides raincoats, boots and tents to Christians who meet secretly outdoors in Russia. Christian broadcasting is done in nine European languages, Chinese and other Asian languages.

1988

Underground church meets outdoors.

Two hundred believers are hanged in Iran and 800 are jailed. Soviet Press confirms our radio work. More than 1000 Dinka Christians massacred in Sudan. VOM workers bring relief to persecuted believers in Mozambique. Couriers from VOM deliver food, clothing and Bibles to hard-pressed believers in Romania. Chinese bishop, Gong Ping Mei, after 30 years in jail, claims official church has nothing to do with Christianity.

1989

Triumphant Romanians remove communist symbol from flag.

A failed attempt at democracy shows the brutality of Chinese Communists as, according to the Chinese Red Cross, they massacre an estimated two to three thousand protesters in Tiananmen Square, Beijing. Eighty thousand copies of John's Gospel confiscated near Karkov in the Soviet Union. Demonstrations begin throughout Eastern Europe and on 9 November, the Berlin Wall is torn down. Romanian pastor László Tökés prays in Timisoara. As the secret police come to arrest him, other Christians gather around the pastor protecting him from the advancing officers. Before long, thousands of Romanians are in the square in Bucharest protesting the oppressive regime of Nicolae and Elena Ceausescu. They have no fear as the soldiers are ordered to shoot the demonstrators. Many of the soldiers, overcome by the conviction of

Aid for Romania.

the people, turn on the secret police. Thousands are killed in the mass hysteria and crossfire. Finally, on 25 December, peace comes to the oppressed nation of Romania. Tens of thousands of Romanian citizens kneel to recite the Lord's Prayer. The Ceausescus are executed. Within a few days of Romania's borders being opened, VOM workers bring trucks and trailers filled with Bibles and aid for the people.

1990

For the first time since Pastor Wurmbrand's arrest, the ministry is able to freely transport help and Christian material to Romania without the threat of imprisonment. It is also during these initial trips that the ministry representatives witness the harsh realities of the tragedies endured by their brothers and sisters throughout decades of oppression. Tom White is invited to take leadership of VOM in America. Richard and Sabina return to their homeland of Romania after 25 years of

exile. They are greeted upon their arrival by hundreds of friends and former prisoners. Before leaving the airport, the Christians, overcome with love, sing joyfully to the Lord. Richard is widely received by many churches and even preaches on public television.

A prison in Romania that once held Pastor Wurmbrand and other Christians, now warehouses Bibles and other Christian literature.

He regrets the execution of the Ceausescus and preaches a message of love and forgiveness. A Christian printing facility and bookstore are opened in Bucharest. The officials of the city offer storage in an old prison below the palace of Ceausescu, the very site where Richard was held in solitary confinement. This is where he dreamed of the possibility of creating this mission. During 1989 and 1990, communism begins to fall in Hungary, Bulgaria, Czechoslovakia, Lithuania, Poland, Russia, Germany and Ukraine. By 1991, Lithuania, Belarus, Yugoslavia and other Eastern Bloc countries are free. Another printing press is uniquely hidden in a rural village of China, producing tens of thousands of pages of Christian literature. In November the International Christian Association is incorporated as the official umbrella of the "Wurmbrand" missions.

1991

A VOM office is opened in Cherkassy Ukraine, where the Voice of the Martyrs newsletter becomes one of the most widely distributed Christian publications in the country. Ten tonnes of literature and aid are rushed to Siberia. On 25 December, Mikhail Gorbachev resigns as President of the USSR. The following day, the Soviet Union officially breaks up. The hammer and sickle symbol is replaced with the flag of Russia, bringing an end to one-party communist rule for the first time since 1917. The ministry increases its work in Saudi Arabia, Cuba, Tibet, Vietnam and Indonesia. Merv Knight is appointed International Secretary of the ICA, to work with the Chairman, Rev W Stuart Harris.

1992

Albania's communist government collapses ending "the first atheist state." On 15 September, VOM opens a Christian bookstore in Moscow. With the newly opened borders of Eastern Europe, VOM is able to distribute over one million illustrated New Testaments to children in Bulgaria, Albania, Romania, Moldavia, Russia and Ukraine. Thousands of used Bibles and Christian books, provided by Christians around the world are sent to northern Nigeria, where hundreds of churches were destroyed by radical Muslims. Christians in Russia are free, but their churches have been destroyed. With help from the German mission Stanislav Forejt opens a VOM office in the Czech Republic.

1993

In former communist Albania, Richard Wurmbrand leads an emotional time of prayer in the palace of Enver Hoxha, the deceased Stalinist dictator. With help from VOM, Stephanus Center, a coffee shop and Christian bookstore is officially

Meeting in Enver Hoxha's palace.

opened and dedicated to the Lord in the capital city of Tirana. Two Vietnamese pastors are released from prison after a worldwide prayer and publicity campaign. Mr Harris chairs his last ICA meeting in 1993 and hands these responsibilities to Paul Gustafson who has chaired the annual conferences of the ICA from 1994 to the time of writing. The first Czech newsletter is published as VOM strengthens it foothold in former communist Eastern Europe.

1994

In October, the ICA commissions a semi-trailer for relief destribution to the CIS and Eastern Europe. New opportunities arise to assist families victimised by

VOM aid for former communist countries.

Shining Path terrorists in the mountainous areas of Peru. Imprisoned terrorists are also ministered to and many come to Christ. VOM sends shipments of clothing and Christmas care packages for children. Kim Il-sung, the president of North Korea dies and is designated "Eternal

USA office in Bartlesville.

President". He is succeeded by the de facto head of state Kim Jong-il. In a continued effort to penetrate North Korea, improved techniques are used to float 80,000 Scripture balloons across the borders. These share our love and prayers for those oppressed by this Stalinist regime, and teach the saving power of Jesus Christ. VOM-USA moves to new office in Bartlesville, Oklahoma.

1995

Richard and Sabina return to Romania to officiate at the opening of the Agape Children's Home, a place for Romanian orphans and street children to receive love, care and the saving knowledge of the Gospel. The home stands as a reminder of the suffering of those who have gone before them. Richard states during the opening ceremonies that the Agape Children's Home was built with the "tears of the martyrs". Bible distribution into China is increased after the Public Security Bureau continues to crack down on unregistered house churches and confiscates all Scripture, even Bibles officially printed by the government-sponsored Amity Press. An estimated 100,000 coats are sent to the VOM office in America as Christian families around the nation take part in the "Coats for Russia" campaign. The coats are distributed, along with Christian literature, to rural areas in Russia, Ukraine, and the Republic of Georgia. Tribal villagers in Vietnam receive Bibles in their own language for the first time. Pakistani Christians begin receiving help.

1996

The "Coats for Russia" Project is held in Australia with over 20,000 garments contributed. The ministry presses on and develops new ministry outreach into the Communist stronghold of Laos and Islamic-ruled Sudan. The Bibles for

VOM Australia sends coats to Russia.

Captive Nations fund is established, bringing a substantial increase in Bible deliveries into closed countries. Additional opportunities allow VOM co-workers to broadcast Gospel programmes into the Middle East.

1997

VOM in the USA initiates the Mission Sudan project, raising funds to provide LifePaks (mosquito net, a Bible, a hoe, plates, cups, pots, and other daily necessities) for thousands of persecuted Christians in southern Sudan. The first complete Hmong Bible is published by VOM and delivered to Hmong in communist Southeast Asia.

1998

VOM helps Christians rebuild churches burned by radical Muslims in Indonesia, and helps families of martyrs. Radio broadcasts into China continue. Help is given to Christian refugees in southern Sudan, after they flee from Muslim terror in the north. Christians in the Maldives, which claims to be 100 percent Muslim, receive help from VOM. A picture received by the mission shows believers in North Korea gathered around a Gospel balloon launched by VOM. Help arrives for Pakistanis whose homes were destroyed by Muslims. Russian underground Baptist pastor, Georgi Vins, who was brutally persecuted in the Soviet Union and was exiled to America in 1979, passes away from illness.

Pastor Georgi Vins.

1999

While the early 90s bring significant changes in the mission activities, there are still considerable challenges ahead. The countries newly liberated from communist oppression remain devastated from decades of terror and neglect and for some years VOM continues a ministry of help and encouragement in countries emerging to a measure of freedom. VOM continues to work in China with its 1.3 billion inhabitants caught in the mouth of a communist dragon. Ministry continues in North Korea, Vietnam, Laos, and Cuba. In India Australian missionary Graham Staines is burned alive with his two young sons by Hindu fanatics. Hindu radicals expand Christian persecution in other parts of India. The Sudan "Blankets of Love" programme begins. VOM helps

Graham Staines with sons Phillip and Timothy.

publish the first Farsi/English parallel New Testament for Iranians. The registered office of the ICA is moved to Oklahoma, USA.

2000

Medical ministry to Pakistan begins. Sabina Wurmbrand dies on 11 August. Christmas Care in Siberia. China approves regulations preventing any group or person to "carry, sell, copy or distribute self-printed or illegally imported religious publications." Team from VOM Australia and VOM-USA distribute blankets and aid to persecuted believers in Sudan.

2001

On 17 February Richard Wurmbrand dies. Christmas Care project begins to help Christian children in Egypt. Reported that more than 250,000 North Koreans flee to China to escape famine. Australian Christmas Care programme in Vietnam. Violent destruction of churches in Nigeria and VOM sends help. On 7 October 2001 Rev W Stuart Harris goes to be with the Lord.

2002

VOM Australian ministry centre.

In Pakistan the worst massacre of Christians since 1947 takes place. Three Islamic terrorists open fire on the Church of Pakistan, killing 75 believers. VOM responds immediately to help the families of martyrs. VOM launches Action Packs as a way for U.S. families to minister to persecuted Pakistanis and Afghanis. VOM Australia moves to new and larger ministry centre.

2003

VOM expands the Action Pack programme to include Iraq. As the war in Iran ends, and at the request of Iraqi Christians, VOM floods Iraq with Christian literature in order to take advantage of this window of opportunity. The Persecuted Church Academic Programme – a dream of Pastor Wurmbrand – is launched in partnership with Oklahoma Wesleyan University. Christmas Care project in Nigeria. Hundreds of believers baptised in China on one day.

2004

PrisonerAlert.com begins and VOM readers write to Christian prisoners in their own languages. Around the world over the next year, more than a dozen prisoners are released. VOM continues to find and help the "forgotten ones" – Christian martyrs who have suffered much for their faith – in Romania and other former communist nations. In Bangladesh, families are attacked by radical Muslims. VOM helps sponsor a children's home there.

2005

The public trial of three Indonesian Sunday school teachers gains international attention. VOM helps the families of the imprisoned women and the church to continue ministry

Dr Rebekka Zakaria, Eti Pangesti and Ratna Bangun.

to Muslims. VOM keeps their situation before the public and in June 2007 they are released. Riots and attacks increase in Nigeria and many churches are burned down. VOM helps rebuild churches, supports Christian orphans and provides widows with grain grinding machines to give them a means of supporting their families. At Kota in India, 280 Emmanuel Theological Seminary students are attacked on their way to graduation. Persecution of Christians in Vietnam intensifies, especially for the 62 ethnic groups like the Hmong, who are targeted by the government. Contact is made with Maciej and Irena Wilkosz from Poland, which leads to founding of VOM in Poland in 2006.

2006

Bibles Unbound begins, allowing Christians in the U.S. to partner with persecuted Christians by mailing New Testaments into restricted nations or hostile areas. China, Egypt, Colombia and Indonesia are the first countries to be targeted with Scriptures. Persecution increases in India as attacks by radical Hindus spring up around the country. In Australia Merv Knight relinquishes leadership to John Wilson and takes on the role of Executive Consultant. He also retires as Secretary of the ICA and accepts an invitation to become the Ambassador-at-Large.

2007

Of the nations where VOM worked in the early years of the ministry, 14 are no longer restricted/hostile. Today they are places where Christians can share and live their faith without fear of physical attacks. In more than 40 restricted and hostile nations Christians still suffer for their faith. Five of these countries – Cuba, North Korea, China, Vietnam and Ethiopia have been on VOM's list of restricted nations for more than 40 years.

2008

With North Korea now under the domination of Kim Jong-il, the balloon launches begun in 1983 continue. Projects to make use of the Olympic Games in China as an opportunity to distribute Christian literature are activated. Existing projects are maintained in the many

Aid for Christians in India.

countries where Christians are persecuted and new initiatives are launched. Hindus attack and kill Christians in the State of Orissa. Fresh attacks by Muslims against Christians in Jos, Nigeria are launched, resulting in at least 200 deaths. VOM continues to pursue the vision of Richard Wurmbrand to serve the persecuted church.

2009

VOM-USA is well advanced with development of new Minstry Centre. In June the Operations Center, first of the new buildings, is opened. On 17 June, in

Aerial shot of 29 hectare development.

his 91st year, Reg Werry, co-founder of VOM in Australia goes to be with the Lord. Christians in Romania organise a week-long Centennial Celebration, held in the cities of Bucharest, Iasi and Cluj-Napoca, to honour and remember the life and work of Pastor

USA Operations Center

Richard Wurmbrand. Representatives of VOM who attend are able to visit the now-closed Jilava prison where both Richard and Sabina

Jilava Prison entrance

were incarcerated at one time or another. They understand the truth of Sabina's comment in years past: "Words cannot describe what it is like to be in prison in Romania." The time to remember the persecuted is now. The Western world is without excuse. The cry of the martyrs has been heard.

The vision remains the same, to *"Remember them that are in bonds, as bound with them . . ."* Hebrews 13:3.

God beware us if we ever cease from caring for His little ones — Sabina Wurmbrand

APPENDIX INDEX

Document I

At a meeting of the INTERNATIONAL COMMITTEE during
our International Conference in Israel (29th March -
11th April 1981) it was recognized that the following
are the main duties of the INTERNATIONAL COMMITTEE.

1) The planing, discussing and advising on international
   tasks.

2) Co-ordination of the finances between the missions for
   these international tasks.

3) Making arrangement for these finances to be audited
   through a neutral auditor.

4) The committee also recognized as its responsibility
   the task to protect the development of the work,
   under the guidance of the Lord and to fulfill the
   mission of the founder, Richard Wurmbrand.

THE MEMBERS OF THE INTERNATIONAL COMMITTEE OF
CHRISTIAN MISSION TO THE COMMUNIST WORLD:

MYRUS KNUTSON, USA
CHAIRMAN

TREVOR MANNING, GREAT BRITAIN

HANS M. BRAUN, GERMANY
GEN. SECRETARY

HEDI FLURI, SWITZERLAND

P.P. JOB, INDIA

MIHAI WURMBRAND, USA

PAT HENEGAN, SOUTH AFRICA

MERV KNIGHT, AUSTRALIA

KLAAS BROBBEL, CANADA

RICHARD WURMBRAND, USA
PRESIDENT

PETER L. GROENEWEG, NETHERLAND

HANS ZORCHER, SWITZERLAND
ACCOUNTANT

Document IIa

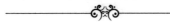

PROTOCOL
:

of the Constituent Assembly of the International Christian Association.

On ..3.11.90....came together in Kreuzlingen, Grenzstrasse 1, by common agreement seven persons in order to discuss the founding of an Association for the purpose of sustaining and promoting certain missionary activities at home and abroad. These persons were: Mrs. Hedi Fluri and Mr. Hans Zürcher of Switzerland, Mr. Hans Martin Braun of Germany, Mr. Klaas Brobbel of Canada, Mr. Jan Bor of the Netherlands, Mr. Merv Knight of Australia, Mr. Thomas White of the USA and Mr. Trevor Manning of England (see also list of persons present enclosed).

Mr. Hans Martin Braun of Uhldingen, Germany, opened the meeting by explaining to the other persons present the purpose and action proposed in order to found the Association.

In response to a motion put forward during the meeting, Mrs. Hedi Fluri of Thun-Schwendibach, Switzerland, was elected Chairperson and Mr. Hans Martin Braun was elected Secretary.

The Chairperson gave the floor to Mr. Merv Knight of Australia, who explained further the idea and purpose of the Association that was to be founded. In particular he drew attention to the fact that the subject had been discussed at previous Assembly meetings and the purpose of the present meeting was to proceed with the founding as intended. All the persons present agreed that the Statutes, which had been thoroughly discussed and worked out in the course of several meetings (enclosure 2) would be approved in the form as laid before them and it was unanimously declared that the founding of the Association had been completed.

All those present declared that they were members of the Association.

Upon the suggestion of Mr. Thomas White (USA), the Association decided unanimously to elect Mrs. Hedi Fluri, Mr. Hans Zürcher, Mr. Merv Knight and Mr. Hans Martin Braun members of the Board of Directors ad interim until the next General Assembly meeting in October 1991, and assigned to the elected members the responsibility in particular for initiating the work of the Association, opening bank accounts and making a study of tasks and responsibilities to be performed.

For the period until October 1991, the accounting firm of Etter Treuhand, Kreuzlingen, Switzerland, was entrusted with responsibility for accounting and the related secretariat work as well as for discharging all formalities required for entry of the Association in the Commercial Register.

Read, confirmed and signed,

Chairperson: Secretary:

H. Fluri   Hans Braun

Kreuzlingen, ...3.11.90......1990

Document IIb

über die konstituierende Vereinsversammlung der International Christian
Association vom ···0·3·Nov.·1990···

Präsenzliste:

Frau Hedi Fluri
3624 Schwendibach
Schweiz

~~Herr Hans Zürcher~~
Postfach ~~1162~~
3601 ~~Thun~~
~~Schweiz~~

Herr Hans Martin Braun
Tüfingerstraße 3-5
7772 Uhldingen
Deutschland

Herr Klaas Brobbel
P.O. Box 117
Port Credit
Mississauga, Ont. L5G 4L5
Kanada

Herr Jan Bor
Postfach 705
4200 AS Gorinchem
Niederlande

Herr Merv Knight
P.O. Box 598
Penrith, NSW 2750
Australien

Herr Thomas White
P.O. Box 443
Bartlesville, OK 74005
USA

Herr Trevor Manning
P.O. Box 19
Bromley, BR1 1DJ
England

Document III

With the collapse of Communism in Eastern Europe and the
increasing challenge of the Moslem world it was considered that a
more neutral title was required for the international work, so
the International Christian Association was registered in
Switzerland in 1990. This is also required for the purposes of
auditing the accounts of the international activities.

It is our strong desire that all the Missions that have been
affiliated with the International CMCW may continue together
under the banner of the International Christian Association.

With a view to the future, when we and others will no longer be
on earth we naturally desire that the whole work including all
the CMCW missions operating and others still to be formed will be
maintained as a united body to further the purposes and aims of
what is often called "the Wurmbrand Missions".

The plan is to continue the regional conferences, so that all
Missions may be able to come together for fellowship and
information.

We ask you, therefore, as we thank God for you and the valuable
ministry which you have conducted and still do minister, that you
will confirm your willingness to be affiliated to the
International Christian association which is now the central body
of "the Wurmbrand Missions".

Please be so kind as to write with confirmation to Hans Braun,
the Executive Director of ICA, PO Box 721, 8280 Kreuzlingen,
Switzerland.

We ever marvel at the miracle of God in the formation of our
Missions to combat Communism, and in response to all the work of
all the missions and in answer to many prayers, we have seen the
walls of communism collapse. Yet God has still greater challenges
both in the remaining countries of communism and in other areas.

The Lord bless you.

Your brethren in Christ,

Richard Wurmbrand,
Founder and President.

W. Stuart Harris,
Chairman of the General Assembly.

Document IV

Bex-11
Glendale
Calif. 91209
Phone (213) 243-5558

PASTOR RICHARD WURMBRAND

Public declaration

Seeing the fact that many persons involved in opposing Communism have been kidnapped by their Secret Police from the West,

that such actions are usually prepared by 1) spreading the rumour that the respective person wishes to go back to the Communist country of his own will 2) by discrediting him in order to make the opponents of Communism to be doubtful and not to protest,

that these preparatory moves have already been made by the Communists and their accomplices, which they have even among important church leaders,

I hereby state in the presence of the undersigned witnesses, that I will never go back to Rumania as long as this is under Communist rule, by my own free will,

that any future declaration of mine in the contrary sense will have been given under influence of doping, threats to members of myk family or other beloved ones and will therefore not be valid. Nobody should give any consideration to such a statement.

I don't go back to Rumania by mu free will. I ask all Christians to protest in case I will have disappeared from the West. I ask them also not to listen to any of the insidious accusations, which come from Communist sources, even if they appear to come from men who seem far away from the Reds, but may be duped by them, unless all the proofs have been given to them and this in my presence in order to give me the chance to show the falsity of these "proofs".

The Communists are masters of deceit. They cannot contradcit my statements and my books about the persecutions behind the Iron Curtain, because I prove them with the Sowjet-press itself. So they have to destroy me physically or morally or both.

I also declare hereby that I am happy and joyous and have not the slightest intention to suicide myself. The Communists have committed many murders in the West, disguising them as suicides or making that the causes should remain undiscovered. If I die in mysterious conditions, it will in any case not be a suicide.

n All the above apply also to my wife, Sabine and to my children, Mihai and Judith.
Glendale, the 4th December 1967

Witness
Deputy General, Dir. of European Christian
Witness   Mission
General Sec. of Mission to Europes Millions

STATE OF CALIFORNIA,
County of Santa Clara   ss.

On this 4th day of December in the year one thousand nine hundred and Sixty Seven

before me, Glenn A. Holtz , a Notary Public,

State of California, duly commissioned and sworn, personally appeared
Richard Wurmbrand

known to me to be the person whose name is subscribed to the within instrument, and acknowledged to me that he executed the same.

IN WITNESS WHEREOF I have hereunto set my hand and affixed my official seal in the County of Santa Clara the day and year in this certificate first above written.

Notary Public, State of California.   GLENN A. HOLTZ

Cranford's Form No. 2—of Acknowledgment—General) (C. C. Sec 1189)   My Commission Expires My Commission Expires Nov. 27, 1970

RESOURCES

The resources featured below have all been referred to within this book by the author.

Tortured for Christ – By Pastor Richard Wurmbrand
194 pages, paperback

The book that opened Western eyes to the persecution that goes on behind the "iron curtain". Over forty years later, this book continues to impact the hearts and minds of those who read it.

Special Edition - 30ᵗʰ Anniversary

Price: $8.00 (Overseas $16.00) Code: B218

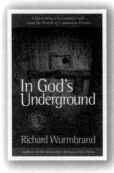

In God's Underground – By Pastor Richard Wurmbrand
276 pages, paperback

In this inspiring drama of faith triumphant, Richard Wurmbrand tells his story of how Jesus Christ met him in the depths of Romania's communist prisons and kept him through years of torture and deprivation.

Price: $17.00 (Overseas $21.00) Code: B102

Serving God in Hostile Territory – By Bianca Adler
110 pages, hardback

As a convert of Richard Wurmbrand, Bianca Adler worked as part of his team in Romania in the 1940s to covertly reach the occupying Soviet troops with the Gospel. She was arrested for distributing Gospels, but the huge bag containing them was never confiscated. "Not one piece was lost or destroyed". Later she served the ministry of VOM in New Zealand for eighteen years. This is her testimony of service.

Price: $15.00 (Overseas $20.00) Code: B150

Voice of the Martyrs has available many other resources to help you learn more about the persecuted church.

To request a resource catalogue, order materials or receive our **FREE** monthly newsletter, contact Voice of the Martyrs today:

Voice of the Martyrs
PO Box 250
Lawson, NSW 2783
Australia

Voice of the Martyrs
PO Box 5482
Papanui, Christchurch 8542
New Zealand

The Voice of the Martyrs
PO Box 608
Streetsville, Ontario L5M 2C1
Canada

The Voice of the Martyrs
PO Box 443
Bartlesville, OK 74005-0443
United States of America

Release International
PO Box 54
Orpington BR5 9RT
United Kingdom

Christian Mission International
PO Box 7157
1417 Primrose Hill
South Africa

RESPONSE FORM

———— ✦✦✦ ————

☐ I would like to receive a **FREE** subscription to Voice of the Martyrs monthly newsletter and receive a **FREE** copy of *Tortured for Christ*.

☐ Please send me more information on how I can help the persecuted church.

☐ I have received Jesus Christ as my Saviour and Lord as a result of reading *Tortured for Christ*.

Name ....

Address ....

....

.... Postcode..

Telephone (daytime) ....

Email Address ....

Please tick the appropriate box(es), cut and mail this form
in an envelope to:

Voice of the Martyrs
P O Box 250, Lawson NSW 2783, Australia